In Celebration of *This Time I Dance!*

"If you're ready to make the journey into the life of living your dreams, Tama J. Kieves is the tour guide you've been looking for. This book is brilliant. It will have a long-lasting impact on all those brave enough to embrace their own magnificence. I simply loved every word."

Barbara J. Winter
Author, *Making a Living Without a Job*

"*This Time I Dance!* is a powerful song for the soul from one who has mastered the steps. Tama Kieves reminds us of the power in dancing to your own music."

Iyanla Vanzant
Author, *In the Meantime: Finding Yourself and the Love You Want*

"There is an authenticity to Tama Kieves's story—a speaking from the heart with feet firmly planted in the soil of daily life. Her story will encourage and give you concrete, helpful suggestions on how you can do the same."

Oriah Mountain Dreamer
Author, *The Invitation* and *The Dance*

"An inspiring demonstration of 'Creating the Work You Love.' Tama Kieves has done it, and she shares it with vibrant authenticity."

Rick Jarow
Author, *Creating the Work You Love: Courage, Commitment and Career*

"Tama gives voice to the fearless spirit within each of us. If you want to wake up to your own purpose and passion, read this book. It will open your heart and guide you home."

Rhonda Britten
Author, *Fearless Living* and *Fearless Loving*

"*This Time I Dance!* beckons one to waltz with the Divine. It will move you to follow your own dream starting right now."

Sonia Choquette, Ph.D.
Author, *Your Heart's Desire*

"Tama J. Kieves writes with real honesty and compassion, and makes a compelling case for the passionate life. Her beautiful book is a great big voice of 'Yes!'"

Gregg Levoy
Author, *Callings: Finding and Following an Authentic Life*

"*This Time I Dance!* is a creative person's Bible! With heart and humor, it illuminates and validates everything you feel when you dare to leave the conventional world to live a more self-expressed life. It really hits home."

Angelique Matney
Principal, The JurisDoctor Career Empowerment
& Transition Support Services for Attorneys

"A compelling and elegantly crafted choreography of one brave woman's pas de deux with her real, true life. Tama J. Kieves tells the story of her creative homecoming in a voice of vibrant passion. Whether you read this book as visionary memoir or pragmatic how-to manual, you'll be inspired and energized to take steps, large or small, in the direction of your dream."

Kathleen Adams, M.A.
Author, *Journal to the Self*

"*This Time I Dance!* is a must-read companion for your journey of discovering and diving into your life's work. Inspirational, yet real, Tama J. Kieves shares her own story in a refreshing, engaging, and warmhearted manner. Both poetic and incisive, she makes transition seem not-so-scary and oh-so-worth-it."

Ann Strong
Transformation coach and founder, Life/Work Resources

"Tama J. Kieves sticks with you like glue. She presents over and over ways to conquer your resistance to doing what you really want. I heartily recommend *This Time I Dance!* to career counselors and their clients."

Judy O'Keefe, M.A.
Career counselor

"Tama J. Kieves understood that name and fame could not buy her happiness. So she took a big risk. She left a life dedicated to pleasing others in order to discover her own life and live it. That choice gave her freedom. It can give you freedom, too."

Paul Ferrini
Author, *The Wisdom of the Self* and *Love Without Conditions*

This Time I Dance!

Sevil —
May you always
follow the one
who dances within you
& always trust your journey!

Blessings —

This Time I *D*ance!

Trusting the Journey of
Creating the Work You Love

~

Tama J. Kieves

JEREMY P. TARCHER/PENGUIN

A MEMBER OF PENGUIN GROUP (USA) INC.

NEW YORK

Most Tarcher/Penguin books are available at special quantity discounts
for bulk purchase for sales promotions, premiums, fund-raising, and
educational needs. Special books or book excerpts also can be created
to fit specific needs. For details, write Penguin Group (USA) Inc.
Special Markets, 375 Hudson Street, New York, NY 10014.

While the author has made every effort to provide accurate telephone
numbers and Internet addresses at the time of publication, neither the
publisher nor the author assumes any responsibility for errors,
or for changes that occur after publication.

Jeremy P. Tarcher/Penguin
a member of
Penguin Group (USA) Inc.
375 Hudson Street
New York, NY 10014
www.penguin.com

First published in 2002 by Awakening Artistry Press
First Jeremy P. Tarcher/Putnam hardcover edition 2003
First trade paperback edition 2004

The Library of Congress cataloged the hardcover edition as follows:

Kieves, Tama J.
This time I dance!: trusting the journey of creating the work you love /
Tama J. Kieves.
p.   cm.
Includes bibliographical references.
ISBN 1-58542-240-1
1. Creative ability in business.   2. Work.   3. Self-realization.   I. Title.
HD53.K534   2003   2002075098
650.1—dc21
ISBN 1-58542-330-0 (paperback edition)

Printed in the United States of America
1   3   5   7   9   10   8   6   4   2

This book is printed on acid-free paper. ∞

Book design by Li Hertzi, Li Hertzi Designs, with Tama J. Kieves

I dedicate this book to that part of myself that inched forward when a thousand winds blew and she had but one small pink birthday candle to hold up her wish. I now dedicate this book and my life to that gleaming one and the one in all of us who listens to the music more than the reproach of the mind—and who dances as if the music were boisterous enough for all to hear—

until of course it is.

Contents

*C*HAPTER FOUR
"So, What Do I Love to Do?" You Ask and Ask and Ask

*C*HAPTER FIVE
Transition Blues and Tender Greens

*C*HAPTER SIX
I Pledge Allegiance to Myself

CHAPTER SEVEN
Every Rosebud Starts in the Mud

CHAPTER EIGHT
Catch On Fire and the World Will Catch On to You

AN EPILOGUE AND A VISION

The Question That Became An Answer

J'm thinking of walking out of the most well-paid job of my life, and I'm not sure that doing what I love—*whatever the heck that is*—will pay bills," I said to my good friend Kir. Though we sat at an outdoor café in the middle of downtown, for me it felt like the end of a road.

My friend slid his mint iced tea to the side of the table and I could see his blue eyes gleam with certainty.

"That's silly, Ms. *Harvard lawyer*," he said. Then he asked me the question that put all the stars back in the sky and turned my "end of the road" into a lavender ladder up to the moon, or a diving board into a garden in full bloom:

"If you're this successful doing work you *don't* love, what could you do with work you *do* love?"

⌒

May this question become your answer—and the beginning of your amazing adventure as well.

An Introduction
and Induction

Pull Up A Chair, My Friend

"So here are some stories to use as soul vitamins, some observations, some map fragments, some little pieces of pine pitch for fastening feathers to trees to show the way, and some flattened underbrush to guide the way back to el mundo subterráneo, the underground world, our psychic home."
Clarissa Pinkola Estés

⌒

"Each of us must make his own true way, and when we do, that way will express the universal way."
Suzuki Roshi

From the minute I began writing this book, I wanted to be an advocate, a champion, a *paper mentor* to those who long to create a livelihood from their natural talents, their dreams, and their love. A mentor stands before us, not with answers, but *as* an answer. They have "been there," faced their own ravaging nights, and now they are here, in the dawn, somewhat intact, and with any luck, dancing. In their presence, our own sense of danger loses a claw or a fang. Then we begin to breathe or even dare to dream in color.

A mentor offers a mug of herbal tea, an oatmeal cookie, and a warm story for every occasion. She says, "Here, pull up a chair, sit down, tell me what's going on with you." She closes the door and opens the chambers of her heart.

So, I invite you to picture the chair with fraying tapestry that awaits you, and perhaps my abundant gray cat will jump on your lap and prod his way into the next dimension. And you will have to summon a pivotal detail, the beam in my eyes, a gleam that says, "I believe in you. I tell you my experiences and stories—my excuse and permission to say, I believe in you. I know you house tremendous power."

Now, of course, I will fling advice as though I know something. But I didn't know a thing at first. My career journey taught me, as yours will contour you. I started out desperate and terrified and convinced I was finally losing my capacity to grope through reality after all. One day I was a fancy-shmancy corporate attorney with a Harvard law degree cruising down partnership track. The next day, while vacationing on a California beach, the rhythm of the crashing waves inspired a slowed-down moment of self-connection, revealing a stunning summons from within. I found myself promising to leave my powerhouse profession and ramble on more beaches, scramble after wonder, get to know myself again—*live* before I died—explore all my imaginable reaches. Needless to say, this seamless "plan" didn't seem too lucid or plausible. I didn't have a rich husband to support me—any husband for that matter—no backup plan, no truly grand faith, and no idea what I would do with an unstructured hour, much less the rest of my life.

Oh, it looks "courageous" now, years into this individualized lifestyle, especially since I can also tell you I ended up a published author and poet, alternative career counselor and creativity coach, even a national seminar leader, and someone whose heart has frequent visitations of faith and conviction. But I began by shivering, questioning, and ultimately questing. It seems that most of us do.

And I felt pretty alone stepping into uncharted territory with the voices of my fears keeping me loud and limiting company. I didn't know anyone else attempting this extraordinary or ridiculous thing called "following your bliss." I ravaged self-help books like a starving person approaches a nine-course dinner. Yet expert after author wrapped up life's dilemmas in three catchy paragraphs, got their lives rolling in those few stylish sentences, packed up the banquet and the mariachi band, and left me still hungry and raw. Everyone between those pages was parading down the main street of their lives, and I still didn't have enough courage to get out of bed and brush my lazy and unproductive teeth. Always, I craved to hear more of the authors' personal stories, their confessions, impressions, what *their* mothers said, and

> I guess I wanted to share the journey, not just the map.

the process that led to their wondrous outcomes and hall-of-fame dream lives. I guess I wanted to share the journey, not just the map.

So I decided to relate the whole enchilada—guacamole, salsa, inelegance, and tears included—so you could see someone just like you, maybe even more terrified than you, go through this astonishing transformation of creating a livelihood from love and from scratch. Of course, I've also included the insights and wisdom I've gleaned from working with hundreds of clients and fellow travelers along the way. And as you read these stories and begin to relax, your own inspired direction will find the way to you.

There's a saying I've always cherished: "You teach what you need to learn." I see that as saying you can hold your own trembling hand by holding the trembling hand of another. And that's why I began writing this book.

Yes, I began this book for a frightened part of myself, but I finished it for a wondrous "us." Because I want to smile at you from deep within. God, when I think about it I want to grin because another bold soul is coming home to herself or himself, dancing. One more kernel of magnificent popcorn is about to pop. So throughout this book—and throughout the splendid stretch of your journey—please imagine my gleaming eyes, sparkling, blazing, and chanting, "Yes! Yes! Yes!"

Oh, yes. Go ahead. You can dance. I believe in you. Oh, and sit down. Sit right here. Push those papers and books aside. Feel free to ask me any questions. Would you care for a cup of herbal tea? I'll be right with you.

Yes, indeed, I will be right with you.

As We Go Forward Together

This book will take you on an experiential journey, a trip through my experience and your own. So since we'll be traveling together, I thought it would be a good idea to clarify a few things before heading out. I hope it makes your reading (and flying) easier.

Artists, Dancers, and Gifted You

I use the word artist a lot in this book and I am not referring only to painters, sculptors, and people who wear smocks, berets, or purple leather boots. I use it in the same way I use the word dancer. To me, artists and dancers are those who *listen to their souls* and express their love and imagination in the world.

We artists and dancers move from inspiration and we will move the world.

We come from all walks of life. We are engineer-artists, secretary-dancers, homemaker-artists, computer-programmer-dancers, poet-artists, realtor-dancers, teacher-artists, and, yes, lawyer-dancers. I'm not singling out an extraordinary species, but beckoning all of us to the shining life of love expressed. I don't care who you are or what your teachers told you. We can all *fly* in the skies of love and creativity.

A Map Of The Scenery

The stories I share are not in order of "the story." I did not write this book in chronological time, but in heart time. In other words, I wrote about whatever experience best illustrated a particular epiphany or movement. But just so you can leap around with me and not get stuck wondering about the order of things, here's the sequence.

After graduating from Harvard Law School, then practicing with a large law firm, I left the law firm to wait tables and explore my love of writing in all its stripes and feathers. I played with poetry, short stories, essays, and magazine articles, and started selling legal writing, magazine articles, and some advertising copy. Some years later, I moved to my dream hideaway in the mountains and began to focus on this book. While living inside this book, I taught adult education classes in creative writing, doing work you love, and living our lives in love instead of fear. My popularity grew, and I offered private seminars and retreats, and began coaching individuals one on one. Today, I lecture, travel, write, and continue to embrace the adventure.

Tools Are Not Rules

The stories that follow are tools to put in your toolbox. Sometimes you will need a screwdriver, and sometimes the pliers in the next chapter will assist you more.

Use whatever helps you. There is no right or wrong way.

At times, you may think the stories contradict each other. To me, they just reflect the wholeness of life. Figuring out when to use pliers as opposed to a screwdriver or a prayer is part of your unique journey, and I wouldn't think of robbing you of the privilege of consulting your own wisdom. My job is to present to you the abundant possibilities.

Also, I share these stories as authentic examples, not scientific formulas. I share the way this creative adventure revealed itself to me. I don't exactly know how your creative adventure needs to take flight. I can't even say if I were to live my own journey all over again, I'd live it in exactly the same way. Creativity defies prophecy and works in its own delightful ways. And gorgeous ones at that!

I begin this conversation with you, in the hope that your heart will leap to its own interpretation, alchemy, and application. I have enormous faith that it will.

Two Suggestions

First, if you've already plunged into your creative journey, you might want to skip ahead to the second half of the book. (Although, the first half of the book will make you feel pretty darn good about your choice!) In fact, this book is designed to allow you to jump ahead or back at any time. Creativity isn't always linear, nor is this colorful journey.

Second, take the time you need to digest each piece. Spend some contemplative moments while you read. Let the sentences roll around in your head. You'd be surprised at the insights that will flash for you or the parts of yourself that will suddenly emerge whole and affirmed. Write down your realizations as they arise. Please write down all your inspirations. *Your* ideas are more important than reading this book.

The Truth

I have changed some names and minor details in this book to ensure the privacy of others. The truth remains the same.

When Life Asks You to Dance, Say Yes!

Chapter One

Okay, my newfound hopeful friend, we begin. I'm not much on small talk, because you and I have too many magnificent items to explore. So pardon me if I just plunge in and presume I know your predicament, even if we've just met and haven't even shaken hands. And by the way, I prefer hugs.

So here's my guess. A secret rattles your core. Some out-lawed prayer for autonomy, mercy, and meaning. And every day you try to put a nice doily over your longing and just go on ignoring yourself like always. Only lately you feel like you're arm-wrestling with a puma just to stay in control and not think those terrifying thoughts about changing your career. No offense, but I'm rooting for the puma. I'm all for the fierce love within you that will not let you settle for rationalization when a life of inspiration calls.

It's More Practical To Be Magical

"You know that emptiness you feel at your job.
It's not emptiness. It's fullness repressed."
A journal entry

⌒

"We are about to break free. We are about to be born.
We have seen the shining. We have seen. We have seen."
Marianne Williamson

I flung that crimson silk cap into the gray Cambridge sky. It would land as a crown, a halo, and a ball and chain. There I stood on the university's soggy lawn amidst flying caps, claps, a thunder of approval. There I stood, eminent and squelched at the same time, graduating *cum laude*, Harvard Law School. Yes, we can muzzle the cry in our marrow, stifle our emphatic hearts, and still soar high. But later we will question the nature of soaring.

For me, later came sooner.

"Just get out of here," my friend said when I told her I couldn't breathe anymore in my office and that if I had to spend another second at Smith & Hudson I might just jump out a window from the thirtieth floor and not return my voice mail.

"Take a vacation. You'll feel better. Go lie on a beach," she said. "We all need to get away."

So I huddled on a beach a thousand miles from my legal career and watched the green waves crash. Damn, I was about to crash, I knew. Maybe, I was also about to crest. Gulls shrieked and I watched the flushed sun steal another day of my life into the horizon. Then the universe hushed into stillness, time paused, and the air seemed to tingle with imminence. And in between the sea's pounding intervals, my heart soared, whispered, roared, "Leave the firm. You can't go back. Honor your yearning to write."

> It all comes down to this:
> We can deny our hearts or
> we can deny our limits.

Instantaneously, my mind began screeching like the gulls harvesting the treats of low tide. "Now you're losing it altogether. You have an office with a view of the mountains. You're on track for partnership. Law degree from Harvard, remember? REMEMBER? You can't just walk out to sit on beaches and write pretty sentences."

How *could* I walk out? What would I walk out to? I didn't want another law job or a wacko, stressed-out killer career. *I wanted another life,* one in which I didn't have to split myself between who I was in my bones and who I was at my desk. Come another ungodly Monday, I didn't want to have to jam myself into pantyhose, pumps, and pretense. My soul cried out for congruence.

I had always, *always*, wanted to write. But I signed up for law because encouraging, well-meaning people told me it would be more practical than starving as a novelist or journalist or we-won't-even-discuss-it poet. And I believed them because they drove nice cars and seemed to have a plan. Besides, I could practice law and write on the side, I reasoned, with the mind of a 22-year-old who thought she could do anything, please everyone, and live forever.

So much for reason and practical plans.

In other words, I had chosen this career out of fear, with the strange conviction that somehow if I worked in opposition to the voice of my heart, I would find security and fulfillment. I fled from rainbows in search of pots of gold. Stifling my passion, I'd hoped for strength and satisfaction. No wonder I only found despair and a tiredness that seemed beyond repair.

Sometime after the beach scene, I did leave my position as a corporate litigator with Smith & Hudson. And I did not seek out another "good and reasonable" job. This time I decided to listen to my heart—not as though it were some crazed dangerous trickster or pipe-dreaming fool to avoid—but as though it *knew* something, and held some fabulous customized direction for me and all the strength I would ever need to follow through. I began with a desperate hope and tenuous curiosity. And on the greatest adventure I have ever known, I ended up discovering not only another way to work, but another way to live.

You can, too.

It all comes down to this: We can deny our hearts or we can deny our limits.

We can choose to be "practical." Or we can dare to be *magical.* But if you knew where your heart could take you, it wouldn't even be "practical" to choose practicality.

Only inspiration offers you a life of passion *and* of safety. There is another way to work. And no other way to choose.

Caterpillar Blues:
No Way Out But Transformation

~

*P*erhaps you feel drawn to weave or teach cooking classes, start that beloved bookstore, or write that software program or screenplay that gleams in the backcountry of your mind like lightning bugs or shooting stars on ink-black summer nights. But then there's the mortgage, the tuition, the Toyota payments, the Visa bills, your age and erratic or esoteric education, and on and on and on—and on. Suddenly it doesn't seem sane to go chasing after lightning bugs when the burdens of reality loom before you like granite mountains and all you have in your pocket are fleeting wishes, falling stars, and tiny wooden pickaxes.

But you have other pockets. And other powers.

It's easy to "see" ourselves as trapped when we listen to fear instead of to inspiration. But through the unlimited energy of inspiration, we possess enough furious love and holy, glowing creativity to realize any dream. *Any* dream. Yet most of us walk as secrets even to ourselves.

Buried in legal briefs and motions as an, of course, overachieving attorney, I couldn't imagine how I could leave "the real world" and live some kind of la-la too-good-to-be-true artistic life or free-bird, entrepreneurial one. I knew I wanted a way out of my crushing career, but I couldn't envision one

Yet doing work you love is the dizzying path of saying yes to yourself and yes to a brilliant, hidden self you do not yet know.

while buried in responsibilities that sapped my spirit and imagination. It's one of those crazy Catch-22s in life. While we say no to the wild love inside us, we live in the dim universe of self-negation. It's hard to see the possibilities when we've said no to our own illumination.

Yet doing work you love is the dizzying path of saying yes to yourself and yes to a brilliant, hidden self you do not yet know. Yes, I will follow my creative instincts even over the thin edge of that forbidden cliff and through the seas and marshes and forests of an emotional, mental, and spiritual transformation. Yes, I will step into the tingling territory that beckons me from beyond. Yes, I will dare to become more than I ever dreamed by saying yes to the dreams that tug at me like spirit children trying to reveal to me another life. After all, this heart-drumming, soul-thrumming vocational pilgrimage is not about changing job descriptions and salaries in the known world. It's about *changing what we know.*

Something in us longs for the impossible because we know it's possible. A caterpillar gazes at a cloudless azure sky with a sense of longing and *belonging.* Yet this low-bellied being cries, "No way, there's just no way I can get from here to there, from the earth and grass of history and familiarity to the sky of delicious flight I ache for." The caterpillar guesses right and wrong at the same time. So do we.

When we look with caterpillar eyes, we can't reach our dreams, can't disregard gravity and the challenges we see before us. We can only scrunch up an oak one inch at a time, years and fears from a blissful sky. Yet the moment you crave that sky, you've recognized the presence of another life within. It is this inspired self that knows the exotic ways of wind and breeze and sudden rampant ease.

Our hearts have called us on to completion and evolution, on to the embodiment of our hidden thirst and ceaseless hunger. The butterfly fluttering within *causing* the stirrings and restlessness will not be stopped by our assumptions and habitual limits. The mountain that obstructs a caterpillar daunts not his winged incarnation. The awakening of the unbounded one within us will awaken panoramas all around us. *The possibilities change as we do.*

⌢

That's why your dilemma doesn't matter. Your bills and bothers and history. Merely problems of perspective. The restrained self will always see a restraining world. The thwarted one can't ever see exalted ways. We who crouch in darkened hallways cannot see the pink of newborn light upon the ocean and fertile landscapes gleaming.

Albert Einstein explained the paradox something like this: A problem cannot be solved at the level of the problem. He could have said a caterpillar will never figure out or handle a butterfly's path. Neither can you. No matter how much you think it all the way through.

Trust the process. A calling calls to remind you to enter the mystery of instinct and the metamorphosis of an inspired life.

Honor your passion to emerge.

Say yes to a supernatural, all-natural self within. Then let creativity transport you to the borderless places, the magical spaces, where caution cannot tread.

This is the ride of your lifetime.

Say yes to this sacred invitation, and let the birth and realization of your life and work begin.

Nothing Stops A Whole Heart

"Love knows no limits to its endurance, no end to its trust,
no fading of its hope; it can outlast anything."
St. Paul, 1 Corinthians

⌒

"Whatever you feed with attention will grow detailed, bold, and
brilliant with life for you. Feed the wolves that howl on the outskirts
of imagination or feed your dreams instead."
A journal entry

One sparrow-boned, average mother in a cotton dress thrusts up a Pontiac Grand Am to rescue a crushed and wailing child. She doesn't think about it. She doesn't analyze how a woman of one hundred and ten pounds who normally can't lift more than two bags of canned groceries can hoist up a ton of Detroit-fired steel. She doesn't think about her own injuries, the heat and fumes, the angle of the steaming vehicle or the medical expenses to come later. Instead, love fills her with her mission: "I've got to save my baby." She succeeds. Her story makes the evening news.

That's how you will do work you love. Your primal heart will override common sense, knock you off your fence, and have you raging and storming *for* your trapped desire instead of *against* its "temptation." Then you will engage the totality of your intelligence to find a means to succeed instead of to tally up and analyze the many ways you could fail.

By the time I left law, I practically couldn't breathe anymore. I sensed my spacious office shrinking, my file folders sulking, smirking, and accusing, and the phones ringing louder. With each passing day, I knew I had to escape that marble-lined, cream-colored elective incarceration.

> Then you will engage the totality of your intelligence to find a means to succeed instead of to tally up and analyze the many ways you could fail.

Of course, I had a thousand and three questions. How will I support myself? What if I can't find another job? What if I'm really not good at writing anyway? What if I ruin my legal career forever and I can never find anything else?

But the day came when I wanted another life even more than I wanted the answers to those paralyzing questions. I guess you could say I had to find a way to twirl a Pontiac on my pinky on a hot summer day, and so I did. It's that simple, and that amazing.

You will never realize your dreams by focusing on passion-sucking, brain-distracting, imaginary, and mutating obstacles. This dream-birthing is not a cool and rational process of sipping iced tea and considering alternatives. Instead, you might say it's the recognition that you have no alternative, want no alternative, and can no longer wait for reason and thunder to catch up with the lightning flashes and clairvoyance of your heart.

Our questions distract us from the realization of our answers. The river can only find the sea by following its inner migration toward immensity. I am not saying that to create work you love, you ignore the challenges and concerns of reality. But I am suggesting that you put those doubts and questions in perspective. Commit to your heart's path, *then* resolve the sticky details. "Do the thing and you shall have the Power," explained Emerson. You know no strength without resolve. The river doesn't kiss the sea by inviting doubts to crumpets and tea.

I once saw a magazine ad that pictured a woman rock climber seizing the edge of an outcropping, her muscles taut with intention. The ad read "You Have to Want It." Her "want" power defied the ravages of gravity, terror, and the unknown strength of the unknown. Yours will too. Nothing stops a whole heart.

Meanwhile, you will always have questions tugging at your sleeves. Reason would have us stand at the crossroads forever.

Live unreasonably.

Decide to live your dreams before you can foresee the means. You can feed attention to your obstacles or you can feed attention to your desire. One gives you magnified obstacles. The other brings you fire.

Fear Uncovers Your Touchstones and Backbone

Chapter Two

So now maybe you want to follow your heart, your bliss, your vocational nirvana, but the hecklers of doubt and cynicism still won't quit.

Super. Fear is a bossy Zen master who swacks you in the ribs to prompt you to sit up straight, concentrate, and penetrate the maddest clarity of your heart.

That's right. Fear won't let you glide on platitudes and other people's wisdom. Fear brandishes a machete to find your loose threads and weak links. Fear asks, how will you eat and stay warm? What will you tell your laughing colleagues and your crying mother? And, hey, why trade a known life for some ethereal promises, anyway? These are some awfully good things to know.

Yet the roar of your heart will quiet all terror. And, sometimes, it just takes a little terror to rouse your heart to roar.

Critics Only Rattle The Rattled

"Do not seek to convince others. Be invincible."
A journal entry

⌒

*"People will say things that sting. They sting more when
I'm raw from my own inner-inquisition."*
A journal entry

Did you get a real job yet?" my mother asked, right after
she'd told me about Mona Rosenthal's Fortune 500 company and
marriage to the plastic surgeon and new button nose. Two thousand miles away, over the phone, I cringed. I felt hot pepper in
my blood; tears welled. Why couldn't my mother look upon my career adventure and say, "You're doing the right thing, everything
will work out, the Force is with you, Luke Skywalker"? Didn't
she know that Joseph Campbell, Deepak Chopra, Marianne
Williamson, and all the other cool gurus tell their minions to
"follow your bliss"? Oh, yes, I spent lots of time blaming my unsupportive mother. That way I could avoid acknowledging and
dealing with my unsupportive *self.*

My mother raised questions that I didn't want to look at.
My mother raised questions I couldn't *stop* looking at. My mother
raised questions that raised the hair on my neck. Her discomfort

with my choices amplified and clarified my own hesitation and concern. I already had a wild woman inside insulting every move I made, cackling at my dreams, ripping the dark loaves out of the oven, and declaring them half-baked. And rather than admit to having this mad woman inside, I'd just get angry at everybody outside of me who didn't immediately fall to their knees in admiration. Anything less than admiration seemed like total annihilation to me.

But criticism only strikes a fire when we provide the wood. It's like Eleanor Roosevelt once said, "No one can make me feel inferior without my consent." It doesn't matter what someone says to us. It matters that *we choose* to listen, agree, and seethe.

Now my mother might have disparaged my plans, deified the lives of others, and actively chosen not to support my decision to dance blind-folded upon the cliff's edge—to dance without some parachute, net, or smitten, rich, Jewish-doctor husband to catch me in the billowing cushions of his bank account. But no matter what she said or didn't say, she could not have made me discredit or assault myself. That's my right alone—and privilege. And I did it awfully well.

In fact, I squandered a lot of energy stewing over other people's opinions of me and insisting that I'd feel better if only *they* could see the light. But these days I believe that everyone who unglues me is a "secret doctor" on a special mission from the universe sent to diagnose a self-inflicted ache within my psyche.

It's best not to argue with those "secret doctors" or seek to change *their* career choices or ability to comprehend your bravery and heroic potential. Wrestle with yourself, if you must, in the privacy of your own mind. Have lunch, dinner, and group therapy with your doubts for as long as it takes to find certainty and harmony within. This can take some time, which is another reason why you'll want to cut short those heated and depleting debates with others.

Years into my current career, I had an experience that showed me the glory and power of coming to peace with myself. At a favorite Chinese restaurant, Richard, the high-strung owner from New York City, came by our table to chat. "What you do for work?" he asked, nodding to me. I told him about personal growth writing and creativity coaching, seminars, and retreats. His eyes glazed over. "She used to practice law," piped up my loving companion, eager to uphold my honor. "She graduated from Harvard Law School." Now Richard stared at me as though I had killed an infant with a butcher knife and had come in gloating over my recreational wantonness. "You no practice law now?" he asked, still staring at me. I tried to shovel in some fried rice so I obviously couldn't talk and might also look like someone who loved his food

But criticism only strikes a fire when we provide the wood.

and would come back often with lots of rich and hungry friends if only he would walk away and not raise his voice again.

My plan failed. Richard's eyes bulged as he saw in his mind's eye the money lawyers effortlessly rake in with their feet up on the desk, as opposed to his fourteen hours a day of sweating oyster sauce and fortune cookies. "What a waste," he said. "What a waste. How your parents feel? You no practice law now? What a waste." I was glad he managed to refrain from spitting on me, dragging me through the kitchen's metal doors and deep frying me, or calling my parents on the spot to address their failure as human beings as well as mine.

Yet, somehow, during this strange scene, I found myself answering Richard's questions with amusement and ease. I noticed the serenity in my belly, a clear lake with not one ripple to disturb its shining blue face. Somehow, I neither crumpled nor blazed at Richard's heated sentiments, the very same opinions that might have once sent me wailing into therapy for months. But I'd already had those demons over for tea years ago and we were good friends now. Okay, so not good friends, but not poison enemies either. Richard couldn't set off a spark in me. I wasn't giving him any wood. All I could think about was how much I cherished my work life, and how I had never once looked back and wished I'd stayed in the throes of my unsatisfactory legal career. Truly, I just didn't have a twig to give him.

That was probably one of the most satisfying moments of my life, like replaying a dream and getting the ending just right. I left that restaurant blessing every therapy bill, every Kleenex, and every "secret doctor" that had unnerved me into self-honesty, self-examination, and claiming my own ground. I had at last become invincible in a quiet, beaming sort of way, because I had finally convinced *myself* of the praiseworthiness of my choices.

And there was no one else left to convince. There never is.

Let people have their opinions, their theories, suggestions, and impressions. Choose not to fight. Live your life.

The lack of self-recrimination answers every irritation.

One Size Does Not Fit All

*"I've been conditioned to value someone else's version of success, but my soul craves **my** conditions of success."*
A journal entry

~

"I saw a car with a bumper sticker that read 'The one who dies with the most toys wins.' I think it should have said joys."
A journal entry

One snowy Valentine's day, I gave a speech at a local high school about self-love and going for your dreams. Greeting my audience, one hundred squirming teenagers, I asked them to identify the most successful person: the doctor, the florist, the auto mechanic, or the poet. "The doctor," responded a tall boy in a black Def Leppard T-shirt. "Anyone agree?" I asked. "Put your hands up." The audience roared with hands. Brainwashed already. A Pavlovian response to the meaning of life. One hundred faces, one hundred backgrounds, one hundred exotic hearts and original minds, and only one way to imagine "success."

Yet despite cultural definitions, the soul still renders its own evaluation. We can dress in Armani and drive a Ferrari and yack to our cronies on our cellular phones. Yet we all answer alone to an arbiter within—not of society—but of the bone. When we close our eyes at night, our contributions in the world will either make us feel hallowed or hollow. The real measure of success is not in our possessions, but mingled in our marrow. Our spirit either feels empty or full, depleted or alive. It doesn't matter which toys we can buy. *It matters what we buy inside.*

While in the process of writing this book, I visited with the Paxtons, some older and well-to-do acquaintances. They welcomed me into their spacious home, embellished with Japanese paintings, hushed privileges, and fragile vases filled with fresh orchids. "So, you're writing a book instead of practicing law," Rachel Paxton said, loud enough for her husband in the football-field-sized kitchen to hear. Suddenly, I felt like I'd said I'd abandoned partnership track to play with Barbie Dolls or toss pink paper airplanes to China or the moon.

Richard joined his wife on the peach-colored loveseat and fingered the gold buttons on his yellow cardigan with concern. "You know we have someone in the family who sold a book," he said and shook his head. "She's a pauper. Never made a penny." Rachel nodded her head in pained collaboration. In other words, the Paxtons said without saying, this distant-kooky-relative had dared the unconventional, just like me, and had failed in broad daylight.

In bed that night, I tossed and turned thinking about that penniless author. How did the Paxtons define pauper? Less than a six-figure income? Driving a red Volkswagen? Still renting? Okay, even if Rachel and Richard knew the history of this woman's bank account, could they know her heart's account? Did she sleep better now? Did she write a line in that book that made her jump up and twirl on her hardwood floors singing, "for this I came, for this I came," to a cracking ceiling and the diaphanous membranes of the heavens? Did her penniless manifesto pave the way for her next book, or maybe her next career, lover, or therapist? I don't know. I had no clue whether she'd say she felt empty or full, bitter or blessed, trashed or transcendent. Neither did the God-like Paxtons. They simply evaluated everything in terms of money. But I looked for the honey.

> It doesn't matter what we can buy.
> It matters what we buy inside.

For myself, I already knew that in writing a book, I might never pull in the bucks to buy a stucco estate near a vineyard or a white Mercedes-Benz—maybe not even a blue Honda Accord with air conditioning or air bags. But I also knew that one day I sipped a bowl of barley soup in the sunshine, in the mountains, on a Wednesday—a former burnout, brain-numbing workday—and scribbled a poem in my journal. And it felt better than any raise, promotion, new account, or congratulation ever could. And better than a trophy car or chunk of jewelry.

It felt sane and whole. With each word I wrote, I felt a sense of completion, of recognition, as though my feet had found *my* ground, my unseen track through this dizzying life, a track that glittered in the sun like cobblestones forged from diamonds. And on this found ground, the clocks stopped ticking and the harried race for God-knows-what finally quit.

I just knew, *I'm there now. I'm there now. I don't need anything else. I don't want anything else. I wouldn't choose another door on "Let's Make a Deal." I wouldn't play any more game shows or games.* In that moment, I felt as though I'd had an adjustment from the cosmic chiropractor and all the parts of my spine slipped into place and hummed with connection and thanksgiving. I just kept humming inside. After that, no amount of "cheese" could tempt the rat in me to ignore my inner direction again. There's just no cheese in that kind of cheese.

What will you live for? What you *look* like to others or what you *feel* like to yourself? Appearance or experience?

I'm not saying you shouldn't buy villas and fresh orchids, or soar to fiscal heights with your web-based business or heart-inspired art. But I am saying the symbols of success don't mean anything to you unless you mean something to yourself. Otherwise, it's like going through life holding somebody else's prizes or driving the latest BMW farther away from your only destination.

Our culture obsesses over image. But our hearts crave reality. You can stand in the limelight and receive the applause, but you can't fake the fullness. The fullness comes from standing in our right lives—not lives decreed by society or family—but lives that express our chemistry, interior hungers, and destiny.

Success is as much a singular affair as falling in love. That's why you can't tell by looking at how well someone's done *exactly* how well he or she has done. Only the soul knows. Only the soul glows. And believe me, when you feel your own "for this I came" moment, the light you touch will be enough. The trappings of success mean nothing to the blessed.

The Living Have No Ghosts

"Things which matter most must never be at the mercy
of things which matter least."
Goethe

~

"How many cars, cottages, and compliments are
worth one chance to live?"
A journal entry

As a litigator at Smith & Hudson, my salary flattered and exhilarated me, yet nothing I would purchase could soothe my private ghost. "What about your dreams?" she haunted. Despite skiing vacations in Aspen, Navajo silver and turquoise jewelry, health spas, and clothing boutique binges, the rattle of her questions would not subside. "What about the *you* you wanted to become?"

Oh, yeah, that. Too busy this week and next. Pink message mountains and manila file jungles on my desk; yellow Post-its crammed with case citations. Demands. Hours and minutes of my breath. Day after day, I'd scrutinize complaints and briefs until my eyes itched, blurred, then tilted toward the misted blue and white mountains outside my thirtieth floor window. This is my time on earth, I thought. Yet I have to down enough jolts of mocha java just to stay awake.

There was something I came for—wasn't there? The wondering gnawed at me, tainted with a peculiar sense of shame, the shame of not *becoming*. One chance to live. Something meaningful, deep in the canyons of my being, I could be doing. "Doing?" the critical voice in my head jumped in. "You should be doing the brief in front of you. Stop asking fluffy, cosmic questions. Grow up. Accept life. You work. You buy a Honda. Later a Benz. You die. Who are you, someone special?"

"No," the ghost moaned. "What about your dreams? What about your dreams? What about the knowing inside you? This life of living on your surface will not complete you."

Maybe I just expected too much out of careers. After all, I didn't sweat in some factory or grope through my days with a swollen abdomen in a country that didn't have enough clean water, much less, caffeine-free Diet Pepsi. "Do you know how hard other people work to earn the money we make in a week?" Alan, another attorney, once commented. He leaned back into his buttery leather chair. "There are worse things we could be doing," he grinned. Still I wondered if there weren't better.

"You're using your writing talents," my mother once assured me, as did others, since I wrote legal arguments and memorandums. But I might as well have been writing prescriptions or directions to a party. Like Picasso painting the deck or garage. Some inner creative clock ticked, clicked, and bonged in my mind.

The sands of the hourglass seemed to pile up an incriminating mountain against me. One life. One chance. Could I risk never writing my poems, articles, and books, not even attempting to approach the palette of the artful life I fantasized? No. I could not face death knowing I hadn't dared to live *my* life. "I'm not ready," I would sob. Maybe I'd throw my appointment book across the room or stomp my non-corporeal foot. "I didn't get my turn."

I maintained this fantasy that, after death, voluminous beings in white robes would display a movie of my life: its meaning, lessons of love, opportunities, with special effects and scriptwriters. I dreaded the knowledge that I could have glided into my vision, clicked my heels three times, two times, even once, but I had *chosen* not to bother. "You were meant to write books," sighed the angel in the fantasy, running the movie. She bowed her head, as her feathers shuddered with my cosmic shock and loss. "We thought you knew."

One day in real life, a connection smacked me between the eyes, in

Only living your dreams can dispel your ghost. Your gnawing is your knowing.

between sighs, in between calculating how many more hours and minutes of law I had to practice before I could retire and crawl off and curl up into sleep.

The angel in the after-death fantasy was the ghost that plagued my days. *I did know. I did know. I did know.* How could I ever feel peaceful again, not devoting my precious resources to the purpose and promise of my life? How could I ever see my time-robbing, monopolizing, and lobotomizing job as "safe" just because it paid well? I felt at risk with every passing second. My heart beat the beat of a writer, while I struggled, shopped, and cried to therapists in the life of an overworked attorney. I did know.

And so do you. Only by living your dreams can you dispel your ghost. Your gnawing is your knowing. On the right path, there is no secret mortification and no phantoms.

We pay our bills, climb our hills, and swoop through our lives with the lyricism of no regrets. No amount of money can buy this essential peace of mind.

No salary ever pays enough for us to leave our truth behind.

Only a life of self-honor feels safe and sure. Everything else leaves us empty, hungry, and haunted for more.

Count On Support You Can't Account For

*"The moment one definitely commits oneself, then Providence moves
too. All sorts of things occur to help one that would never have
otherwise occurred . . . unforeseen incidents and meetings
and material assistance, which no man could have
dreamed would have come his way."*
Goethe

~

*"Now I've begun to think that it's not that the universe supports us,
but that it supports itself. It provides conditions of growth and plenty
when you step into the role it has in mind for you.
Nature doesn't support the journey of a cactus in the rainforest.
But things come easy to the palm."*
A journal entry

I'd gobbled up shelves of self-help books that swore that if you
pursue your dreams, "the universe supports you." Events line up,
angels pamper your path, and circumstances generally turn peachy
and paranormal. Well, I welcomed universal support, actually any
assistance from anywhere, but wondered if sane people balanced
their checkbooks on celestial promises. Could I rent an apartment
and buy Starbucks coffee on divine benevolence? Could anyone
traipse after sparkles and pay their car insurance premium at the
same time? Did following my heart make me special?

Apparently so.

Life just turns deliciously quirky when you stop resisting yourself and, instead, honor the intuition that tugs at you like a puppy on a leash in the park. Follow the magic and magic starts to follow you. Love boldly and tectonic plates shift. It's a kinder zone. You are not alone. In this co-creative realm, helpful circumstances will often show up like breadcrumbs and markers on the trail home.

Scholar Joseph Campbell put his findings this way: "I even have a superstition that has grown on me as the result of invisible hands coming all the time—namely that if you do follow your bliss, you put yourself on a kind of track that has been there all the while, waiting for you." We don't have this kind of exotic experience when we swallow our dreams—only when our dreams swallow us.

Let me give you an example. After a few years of poking around with different kinds of writing, I decided to write this book. And as I resolved to put aside all other writing and write this book, I imagined tucking myself away in the foothills outside the noise and demands of city life. Devoted writers always seemed to have alpine hideaways in the removed and serene places of inspiration. But my soul's urging seemed more like wishful thinking as I started researching the possibilities. I lived on very little money at the time. And as the scenery turned beautiful, the leases of even the smallest cubbyhole soared as high as the rugged evergreens I wanted outside my window.

So I turned back, defeated, and ready to live in the "real world" of limitations. My inner critic scoffed at me and roared at my Walden-type fantasies of feeding squirrels and woodpeckers, and the neglected wells of my creativity. "You could afford a place in the mountains like you could afford a house on Jupiter," it howled in uproar, and slapped its bony, brittle knees.

"Well, are you ready to move to the hills?" my friend Lucy said over coffee at Denny's one day. She grinned. I grinned and waited for the punchline. Not in the mood for jokes though. "Well are you packed?" she said, then bubbled the news. Time slowed down like one of those melting Dalí clocks, and I watched the words trickle from her mouth like diamonds and emeralds. I will always remember that feeling of eerie delight, of getting exactly what I dreamed of without struggling at all. Spooky and sublime.

Six weeks after the Denny's moment, I found myself stowed away in a one-bedroom apartment with a backyard of Ponderosa pines, flax and bluebells, deer, butterflies, magpies and magic. My best friend lived next door, and together we sipped tea on her sundeck and discussed writing while indulging in hummingbird visitations and some pink, peach, and amber sunsets. I have to say the scenery on Jupiter was even better than I thought.

So how did these improbable circumstances pluck me out of my resignation? Lucy had moved to Indian Hills and met Jane, an athletic elderly widow who lived up the road with an English sheepdog, pictures of her children, and a separate ground level "mother-in-law's apartment" where her oldest son used to live. Jane had never considered renting the empty space to strangers. But after a conversation with Lucy, she decided to let a "quiet writer" keep an eye on her, live downstairs, and pay less than two hundred dollars a month. Gasp. Pinch me. Those improbable and celestial self-help books had been right. I had "manifested" my desire, the setting my dream required, served up by an invisible butler.

"Don't expect things to come to you on a silver platter," the cynics say. But today I say, Oh, do. Do expect what you can't explain. Do expect what you can't believe. Do expect goodness to spill from all corners of your life the instant you turn that corner and choose to honor the magnetism of your heart. You may have had to claw and grapple to create a life that barely felt all right. But once you listen to the larger direction within you, you stop swimming upstream, and the flow of life changes in your favor.

> Okay. Coincidences, luck, providence, cosmic "woo woo," voodoo or grace, *something unusual* happens when we choose to follow our inner connection.

Suddenly our desires aren't in the way of our productivity. They *are* the way.

And just in case you're wondering, this current doesn't only favor people who do Hatha yoga or chant with quartz crystals or donate money to environmental agencies. You don't need a religious orientation or a cheery disposition. You don't have to be Wayne Dyer, Mary Poppins, Yoda, or Shirley MacLaine. Just you, you with a mind full of shadows and a lantern of a heart.

For some time, I ran a monthly "Do What You Love For a Living" support group and every month some attendees—awe streaking their faces like a meteor shower—would share an experience of a situation taking a turn for the sublime and "just working out." Even Evelyn, an engineer, hardy in her faith of being faithless and pedestrian. "Well, I never thought *I'd* say this," she began one Sunday, "but something's just pulled some strings for me." Evelyn had just inherited money from a distant aunt in Spokane. She had learned of this news precisely one week after she had decided to "risk it all" and return to school to study interior design.

Many scoff and say, yeah, sure, coincidence. Okay. Coincidences, luck, providence, cosmic "woo woo," voodoo or grace, *something unusual* happens when we choose to follow our inner connection. Something gives, and fortune smiles upon us like an indulgent grandmother offering lemon drops and candy kisses from a secret stash. And wouldn't "reason" insist that we acknowledge patterns and facts, even if they challenge our sense of logic?

This mystery is waiting to champion you in ways you will never, *never* imagine. Stop swimming upstream splashing and kicking to bitterly grasp an existence of compromise and forbearance.

Step into the river.

Trust the unseen networking of all of life. Those invisible operators are standing by to take your call and place your order.

Life does work in your favor, when *you* do.

⌒

Sometimes You Have To Lose The House
To Acquire The Mansion

⌒

"The spiritual life is not a special career, involving abstraction
from the world of things. It is a part of every man's life;
and until he has realized it, he is not a complete human being,
has not entered into possession of all his powers."
Evelyn Underhill

*I*nsecurity led me to the boldest security of all. Without a stable job, a husband to support me, an oil well in my name, or a joint account with Rockefeller, I had to find another brand of safety. Fast. And while I thought I needed money, The Great Protector, to be okay, I found out what I really needed was *me* to be okay. I had to work with this frightened animal I call my mind and finally harness its frantic power in my favor. I had to allow my tiny heart to blossom into its tremendous capacity for bravery, self-compassion, and a radical faith I never imagined. Believe me, nothing calls us to penetrate our full faculties like raw freedom. And I assure you that the security you realize then runs deeper than deep pockets.

Maybe it's just that when everything we know doesn't work, we start searching for what we don't know. As I transitioned out of my familiar community of stressed-out, downtown lawyers, I gravitated towards Kir, a free spirit with long hair, a crisp wit, and a gentle smile. Okay, he even wore beads. To a Jewish girl from Brooklyn, raised on catastrophe prevention and worry as a way of greeting the day, Kir had a startling approach to the world: relaxed.

My new friend had studied meditation for close to twenty years, burned Nag Champa incense and sage sticks, and intuited guidance, dreams, and the watercolor language of the soul. He laughed when I told him I didn't have a 401(k) plan, which to me, meant I might die or fall into the tar pits of the reckless. Kir's sense of security wasn't tied to an external circumstance or predictable tomorrow, but to the love in his heart and the trust he had in each moment. In his presence, I felt a kind of spaciousness, like an ocean forever rolling into a soft, blue horizon. I'd never experienced such assurance and ease, not even in the people I knew who had cleaning ladies, personal masseuses, reserved pews, and bank accounts as solid as oak trees in the sun.

Kir attributed his peace and his sense of connection to a sentient wisdom within and to a friendly, interactive universe playing harmony to his melody, supplying delicious coincidences and whispering love songs to him whenever his mind whimpered in the darkness. This sounded crazy to me at first, but appealing. And somewhere deep, deep inside, it must have stirred a breeze. Because whenever I got scared about not having control or clarity, which seemed to occur in two-minute intervals, I binged on the comforting and invigorating books Kir suggested.

I explored "imaging" my desires through visualization, replacing negative beliefs with loving ones, and meditating to temper the temper tantrums of unsolicited thought. Soon I was going through books like a library on fire. I wanted to walk down all the sacred paths to freedom. The world expanded for me. Everything I read told me external security wouldn't save me and that peace of mind only came from within. Brain researchers and gurus, Mother Teresa and Deepak Chopra, Ann Landers and the Buddha, rabbis, mystics, meditation teachers, preachers, and psychologists all hummed the same tune in slightly different keys. I guess I'm one of those people who learns through repetition. Because I started to believe that I needed peace and trust even more than cash.

Yet I found more strength in swinging from vine to vine than I ever would have huddled away in a life-proof life.

Still, as I explored these back roads of reality, I kept reassuring myself that I had both feet on sound ground and wouldn't trek to Tibet or ascend to the astral planes anytime soon, though I might fly out to California to take a workshop. Now, I never did see white light or follow my breath long enough to hear the music of the spheres or voices or whatever you're supposed to hear if you can shut your mind up long enough to have a pure gateway-type experience. But a funny thing happened along the way. As I opened my mind to new possibilities, new experiences glided in.

Something clicked. I began to feel connected to a "knowing sense," a deeper part of myself that did not doubt or waver, even when the circumstances of my life looked more like confetti in a hurricane than a path to a goal. Somehow I understood that if I trusted what I felt instead of what I could prove, this unseen strength would sustain me and always had. Money and praise had never given me this kind of breathing room with events and relationships. Finally, I didn't have to tap dance when fear entered the room. I was learning to tap into a feeling that could embrace both my fear and me, and keep my precious vessel afloat at sea. Now I knew why Kir walked in freedom with an even heart. It's one of the great ironies of life: the more faith we have in mystical realms, the more ease we have in a material one.

Your heart has called you to step out on the edge, the thin ground that is actually safer than all you've known before. Trust your instincts instead of your conditioning. The edge will bring you to *your* edge and to the secret dimensions within you. This alone is worth the journey.

I remember how I used to whine to friends about how much I needed a whopping trust fund, a pipeline of endless cash to do my dreams. Yet I found more strength in swinging from vine to vine than I ever would have huddled away in a life-proof life.

Because I had to search for a sense of safety beyond dollar, privilege, and approval, I inherited the ultimate trust fund. I learned to trust in my own resources and the startling generosity of life. I learned to find steadiness and loving confidence even in the wind and the rain, the uncertainty and the pain.

You will, too. And there is no other security.

Creating Time for the Time of Your Life

Chapter Three

*O*kay, so now we've covered most of the blocks that come up before you even let yourself consider a dream. But then there's still this inertia thing. You know, "I'd leave my job in a heartbeat, if I knew what else I wanted to do." Thump. The ball drops. No lasting focus because you don't have the time. **Your job has your time.** The foul monster is shredding hours and weeks in its rotting, dream-stealing teeth even as we speak.

Draw a line. Take back your time. You can't wait for your heart to bloom with a vision in the middle of days teeming with madness and maintenance. Nothing flutters into a cluttered life. The frantic and exhausted mind does not possess the energy to inspire a love-filled path. But you can find a way to curb or flee the madness. And when you do, your dream can find its way to you.

It Takes An Intermission
To Give Birth To A Mission

"Vision doesn't come courting in cramped places.
She can't get her head through the door.
I have found that inspiration is a particular visitor."
A journal entry

"You can't cling to the old nest and soar to the flowering
branches at the same time."
A journal entry

I thought I could wait until I was inspired by some other life
choice in order to leave the job that dampened my spirits daily. I
thought that maybe one day I'd be standing by the water cooler in
the middle of the hallway and suddenly I'd see it all, the Grand In-
struction Book from The Most Loving Universe, opening before
my eyes. And then right in the middle of an ordinary day, with too
much traffic on my way in, too much work to do, too much coffee,
and much too little sleep or primal scream therapy, I'd instantaneously know just how to create some new mythological career
life. Now there's a dream for you.

That's like deciding not to go to the dance and expecting
Prince Charming to materialize in your kitchen instead, where
you're stirring green beans and waltzing around with some dude

named Mr. Clean. But regal boy doesn't make house calls and neither does inspiration. Unfortunately, we have to leave our prisons to find the keys to our freedom. Look, I'm not making up the rules. I've just noticed that we only tend to find our mission once we take an intermission from the work life that doesn't work.

You have no idea how much your current job affects your thinking about your future and keeps you chained to your past. On vacation from my law firm, I got a suntan and what seemed like a brain transfusion. I sprawled out on a beach and listened to the waves crash. I watched Californian teenagers swack volleyballs and hoot with sun-drenched abandon. Suddenly I began to see that outside of my office, not everybody scowled and snapped and neither did I. Only when the fury and ache of my frenzied career life started melting from my muscles could I even begin to imagine a life of freedom and ease. I had honestly forgotten what peace could feel like. Those ten vacation days spawned a startling perspective: *I could not assess my job and my life while in the thick of the job that was my life.*

Take a friend of mine, Carol, for example. She's fed up with word processing at a large law firm. But she can't imagine another way to live. She has no burning love she knows of, lots of figments of possibilities, butterflies all flitting in the periphery of her mind, but no deep convictions, no "path" that bears her scent, her name, or even her initials.

On weekends, she buys the latest career search and "do

your dream" books. She flips through one at night, after a particularly savage day at work. The book suggests writing exercises and goal setting. Carol yawns. The words leap up and down on the page like Mexican jumping beans making a trampoline of her exhausted, threadbare brain. Carol has worked hard enough for the day. She flicks on the television instead, just for a moment, and watches a sitcom with a laugh track and a safe, obvious, no-brainer plot, so unlike her life. Passivity sinks in like ether, and a minute becomes the evening and then some.

"Great," she thinks, "I can't even get myself to do one exercise. How will I ever create a whole new life? I probably don't have the commitment and the drive. Maybe I'm lucky to have the stupid job I have." But Carol forgets what she feels like when she hasn't worked all week in an environment that demands she hold her true nature in high security check as though she secretly contained plutonium. She has denied herself for so long that she can't exactly remember what it tastes like to express herself, honor herself, embody herself. Carol forgets what it feels like to feel interested, engaged, rested, centered, and once again *connected* to an incandescent composition of life. That's why Carol needs a "time out" to recover from her own self-misuse, breathe big, rest large, and recall the forgotten strength that can accomplish what seems impossible to an exhausted and denied self.

> I've just noticed that we only tend to find our mission once we take an intermission from the work life that doesn't work.

So do you. You need a space in your life to delve into the dimensions where your budding answers enjoy a climate in which to bloom. You are about to begin an incredible pilgrimage. Changing jobs is a piece of cake. But changing lives *takes* the cake. After all, a calling or life's purpose isn't about circling want ads. It's about asking yourself, at the deepest level, what you want. What do you ask of this lifetime? A question that brings to life a hundred other questions, a hundred other flashlights suddenly beaming into the secret tunnels of our consciousness.

Who are you? What do you believe you can achieve? What do you believe you deserve? Can you trust yourself? Can you trust the world? I doubt you can respond to these questions on your lunch hour, while picking up the dry cleaning, visiting the post office, calling your husband (who, of course, wants to tell you what's wrong with managed care), and chewing each bite of your turkey sandwich about a thousand times like skinny people in diet books advise.

After what I called my "revelation vacation" in California, I resolved to take three months out of my life to reexamine as many options as I could. To finance my transition, I lowered my expenses, spent some retirement money, and took on part-time work. I also decided that if in three months I felt no closer to clarity or the creation of my dream, then I'd go back to "real life," lay down my griping, forget about this crusade for a utopian career-life, and just do it the world's way once and for all. Three months turned into six months, six months into a year, and eventually I started selling some writing and teaching classes. I have never since entertained the idea of going back to a less expressed life.

A friend of mine couldn't leave her full-time work. So instead she began using her weekends to research the idea of opening up her own boutique. Meanwhile she squirreled away money for her "escape route." More importantly, during her workweek, she no longer stayed late or said yes to extra or last-minute deadline assignments. As she put it once, "I do what I have to do without giving away my soul anymore. I've given up my attachment to this job. I'm saving my energy for what I really want." You might say she took her time out while still putting time in to a necessary livelihood.

I don't know how the creative self within you will finagle and finance your intermission. But I know you have a thousand options. And the how is not important. Once you decide that destiny is not going to keep its date with you at the water cooler, you can manage to tear yourself away from the life that is standing in your way.

Do it. Find a way to take time out.

All you have to do is take a time-out and honor the purpose of that time. I swear.

Then inclinations start to tap you on the shoulder. Then dreams. Then means. Just clear the space.

Consciously let go of what tires you. And what inspires you will take its place.

⁓

Sometimes You Serve Onion Rings to Serve Your Journey

"And this time, I swear, my next career decision will be a heartfelt response instead of a knee-jerk reaction."
A journal entry

⌒

"'But you're a lawyer,' my ego shrieks, as though I had signed some secret pact along the way that declared that henceforth I would only take careers of especially grand self-importance. Except, I reason to myself as any good lawyer would, that I went to law school to increase my opportunities, not to limit them."
A journal entry

*M*ost of us will need a monetary lifeboat. Your lifeboat isn't a way of life, but an *ad hoc* vinyl vessel that somehow helps cross you over into an economically sustaining creative life. I often suggest leaving behind your real job and securing a "drop-out" job, work that covers some expenses, maybe not even all your bills, but definitely, definitely, definitely does not consume or define you. You want something transitory and loose, not another noose that constricts your identity or steals your brand-new fealty.

I waited tables most evenings during the week and bought myself daylight hours to walk in the park, write in cafés, and pray to the bliss gods that I could someday soon find meaning and cash in the same place. I took hours to journal and read and *feel* and peel off the dead layers of yellow skin around my heart and intuition. Self-discovery was my new career and, like any infant, it drew my undivided attention and tickled and drained me just the same.

I chose to wait tables because it sounded free-hearted, like juggling or moon walking, and of another world than corporate law, like traveling in a dark foreign continent, only just down the street. I liked the idea of hiding out and healing, working desk-free, and carrying a tray of Cokes instead of people's hopes and the globe on my shoulders. At last, I had a job that I felt free to lose, permission from myself to take work without taking some holy vow inside myself to be the best thing that ever happened to this joint, to this industry, and to mankind itself—even if I had to give my mere life in the process. Of course, I had to keep reminding myself that I didn't need to make wine cooler salesperson of the month or restaurant manager or owner. I wanted to own my life instead.

At the Paradise Cafe, I could flaunt hoop and feather earrings and hot-pink "I am not a lawyer" lipstick and swish to eighties music on the jukebox as I delivered curly fries, iced teas, jokes, and brownies. And if the day came when I forgot to bring out the guacamole with the nachos or even dropped a plate, nobody filed a civil action or a malpractice suit. My job just wasn't all that crucial. And for once in my egomaniacal life, that didn't seem degrading, but liberating. Because for every notch of status I gave up, I gained a world of freedom.

⌒

Sure I battled with a bruised ego wanting to bruise back. "How could you wait tables with a Harvard Law degree?" it squawked and badgered. "Darling, this is just beneath you, below what you *know* you're worth. Did you just go through the trouble of studying contracts and antitrust law and passing a bar exam so you could serve chicken fingers with honey barbecue sauce?" But I *wanted* to serve chicken fingers. Because I didn't want to linger in the corporate world anymore just to prop myself up while I dragged my soul down. I'd rather bring out onion rings.

At last, I valued self-respect more than self-importance.

"But it's easier to get another job while you still have a job," well-meaning colleagues warned with knots in their voices and blackness in their eyes. They meant switch from corporate to environmental law or to a smaller law firm. Or join the legal department of some corporation or administrative agency. They did not mean waiting tables: touching other people's food and taking orders. They did not mean work in which you didn't need a curriculum vitae or an Armani suit. They meant stay in the game. By all means, stay in the game. Even hide in a Jim Beam bottle, but stay full throttle.

But I couldn't. My head spun as I considered calling other law firms. My vacation at the beach sprawled across my mind—the freedom, the peace, and finally the time to stretch inside myself and touch the hems of life's most important considerations. Did I want to leave Smith & Hudson just to give my body, time, and mind to another firm? Just change letterheads, secretaries, water coolers, and the leading ladies in the inter-office gossip and drama club? Would I ever get another chance to take a break from law if I buckled down again in another firm? "No, no, no!" a voice cried in my head. *"Do not secure your future without securing your intentions. Find out what you want."*

I was tired. I couldn't imagine interviewing again, glittering and grinning, selling someone on how much I loved and craved the law, those long hours of researching the technicalities of civil procedure and other mind-numbing feats of advocacy. Working hard to embed myself in an employer's authority and grace when all I really wanted to do was run for the hills, weave daisies in my hair, and watch clouds and butterflies, and stare at air.

> I didn't want to linger in the corporate world just to prop myself up while I dragged my soul down. I'd rather bring out onion rings.

No, another career job, a situation that "counted" would destroy me. I needed to "drop out" from the professional world for a while, take space, take stock, and understand how I "did everything right" and still ended up so wrong. I didn't want to leap from one wrong choice to the next and call it being sensible. So I filled out an application to wait tables, over-and-under qualified at the same time, and waited at the bar and fidgeted with a lime. The cute, young, party animal restaurant manager read my resume and looked at me as though I had just told a joke without a punch line. Yet in a spontaneous act of mercy or blatant curiosity, he smirked, shrugged, and hired me anyway.

When I walked into the Paradise Cafe and learned how to garnish drinks and peddle appetizers, a reckless feeling hit me. I was not "on track." Like never before in life, this time would not lead to a degree, a license, a bonus, or a bone. Now I could face myself instead of race ahead. I could explore and nurture my talents without having to sell them before their time. I now had time. I'd secured an adequate lifeboat, the kind of job that would carry me, but not tarry me with temptation or self-inflation. I would save my dearest cargo for my final destination.

It's Never A Step Down To Step Ahead

"If I cut corners here, I might just turn some
new corners in my life."
A journal entry

⌒

"Downsizing my expenses is actually starting to become
meaningful to me instead of just demeaning."
A journal entry

*W*hen I chose to put my inflated living expenses on the diet of their lifetime, I had to combat feelings of poverty, discomfort, humiliation, loss, and fear. I couldn't help but feel strange paddling downstream in an upwardly mobile society. I also secretly feared that I might get my canoe stuck in lower ground and never see those bountiful high waters again. "You have to find another way to look at your choices," a good friend reminded me, sounding awfully like Dial-a-Guru, but also like the music of the spheres to my ears. "It's up to you whether you see liberation as exciting or terrifying. You can see transition as some kind of failure or some kind of adventure."

That wisdom carried me a long way. When I ran into tough decisions, I decided to at least attempt to "adventurize" my life, see the heroism in my choices, recognize and support the woman of courage who would stalk her dreams at any cost. From my adventure perspective, I turned each difficult situation into nitty-gritty proof that I indeed dared to walk the walk of a "real writer" or a serious creative pioneer. Gradually, I no longer saw myself as stepping down from a superior life, but stepping *ahead* into a life of artistic dignity and determination.

> Gradually, I no longer saw myself as stepping down from a superior life, but stepping *ahead* into a life of artistic dignity and determination.

When I first left law, I stayed in my same apartment, but later I knew I wanted to shrink my expenses instead of my opportunities. For weeks, I scanned the paper's ads for places to live. I needed a cheap place to prolong my freedom from full-time, high responsibility work. I kept reminding myself, "The fewer dollars I have to pay, the more time I have to play." That sort of mantra helped me as I looked at my share of homes with animal residue you could smell despite the oh-so-attractive orange shag carpet, and cigarette-smoke shrouds emanating from the congenial landlord.

But one day a classified ad for a studio apartment in Capitol Hill jumped out at me. I knew Capitol Hill was a patchwork quilt of a neighborhood made up of young professionals, musicians with green hair and handcuffs, the eclectic affluent in stately turn-of-the-century mansions, and all around open-minded, anything goes, live-and-let-live types. The ad that caught my eye was headlined "Artistic Spirit" and described a large studio of Victorian vintage and charm.

When I first laid eyes on the apartment on 14th Street, the space, or lack of it, unnerved me. One room and the kernel of a kitchen and a bath. Still, one charming room, with vaulted ceilings, antique light fixtures, and a polished oak floor. My contemporaries were probably buying their second homes, four bedrooms with skylights, sunken living rooms, and landscaped yards that would accommodate children, horses, golf courses, wedding parties, and the impromptu runway for a private plane. Meanwhile, I was considering a place a college student would find cramped.

Yet it gleamed.

Suddenly I imagined another Tama, an "artiste" consumed by her work of words, feverishly typing at a keyboard into the sweet, solo hours of the evening, like a prima ballerina pounding her muscles into grace, her sweat into transcendence. I imagined meeting this woman at a coffee house, she with wild hair, purple wool vest, black boots, and an unapologetic face with clear, clear eyes. I'd listen to her story, my café mocha turning cold and my heart warm. How she rented a funky studio in the "people" part of town so she could devote herself to her craft, the spinning of words like threads on a large resplendent loom, color, mesh and weft, all from the never-ending spools of her mind. "I don't have much room to waste time in," she might say. "I don't lounge on the couch, rearrange the shoe racks in closets, or clean out the basement. I do the work I came to do. I live in my creativity, a very sweet mansion."

⁓

How I'd envy her fierce intensity, her conviction, her steely center, and the thick skin of eccentricity that sheltered her from the leering and sneering opinions of others.

In real life, the landlady, an older woman named Darlene who reminded me of a slightly rumpled pigeon, babbled on about how much closet space and storage the place had and how I could use the washer and dryer in the basement. The sun streamed in like chords of music from the ten-foot windows, the apartment's glorious attraction. I imagined the commitment such a terse nest would demand of me. It suddenly seemed to me that I had come upon my own private monastery. For whatever the place lacked in physical dimension, it would make up for in the enormous spree it could grant my soul.

As I looked around, I imagined another Tama, an aging lawyer, with calm and character etched into her face. "Oh, I've lived a bit," she might say, self-satisfaction rich in her voice. "Even did a stint as a writer. Did it right, too. Rented a small place smack in the center of urban culture. Drank coffee in cafés right in the middle of the day. Impeccable fun. Sure glad I did it while I was hopped up enough and chock-full of possibilities and questions. Quite an experience, too." Then she might have traveled throughout the country or world, and explored the rain forests or a rainbow of other careers, as she gratified all the wayward children of her curiosity. In other words, she would have browsed at the greatest department store of all—life—tried on any outfit that suited her, and experienced no lack whatsoever.

Yes, this modest living space held the promise of adventure, like a great steamer leaving the shore of the known landscape or a trek through terrain beyond the guidebooks where tourists never enter. Here, I would wade into the thick of my experience instead of standing on the sidelines imagining, but never getting my life past just passing thoughts. My eyes toured the room and landed upon the spot where I could set my computer. I imagined spider plants and jades and Swedish ivy drinking in the sun from those proud and fantastic windows, a cat or two soaking up the abundant warmth and light and mystique of my creative spells. Either of the two Tamas I had imagined would have lived in such a place, worked here, reclaimed a part of her soul here, and sailed into the next horizon from this efficient port.

"Well, have you made up your mind?" Darlene asked, eyes bright with the prospect of renting to a former lawyer rather than a crack dealer or drummer whose latest band called itself the "Dead & Rotting Pigs." With my heart pounding and my future quivering, I resolved to plunge into my self-proclaimed adventure and dare to leave furniture with friends and pack books and vases into storage, rather than keep living in storage myself. "Yes," I said. "I'll move in during the weekend."

A heroine was born. I had just lowered my rent and raised my standards.

Full Hearts Inspire Fit Budgets

"I don't want to sacrifice my lifestyle. Oh hush, little one, a life of spirit and substance will outstrip a life of style. You lust for excess because you have deprived yourself of marrow."
A journal entry

⌒

"It is life near the bone where it is sweetest."
Henry David Thoreau

*M*aybe you think that cutting down on material consumption sounds like restraint, deprivation, limitation, a lock and key on your financial liberty. But get ready to *undo* limits. This path is about real freedom—not just the "freedom" to be rash because you're bored and you have cash.

Relax. You won't have to hold yourself back from what you want.

Instead, when we gravitate toward the dream we *really* want, the feeling of completion feeds our covetousness and stimulates our health. Then, we naturally turn away from inadequate extravagances because vanity, excess, and insanity no longer feel like wealth.

Packages. Packages. Packages. I remember dumping May D&F and Fashion Bar bags and cardboard boxes on the bed. Crinkling plastic and rustling tissue paper. The aroma of novelty. Yet another shopping spree, a seductive exuberance about to subside. Did I need this new mountain of silk scarves, shoes, more blue silk shirts, and another gray suit? Well, yeah, about as much as I needed designer underwear, *more* designer underwear. But in the moment, the mountain of fashion softened my ache and boredom. The allure of new, more, better. Though not enough, because life, itself, was not enough; days and weeks and months were just too much like driving a beige car on a highway that didn't take me anywhere— despite the well-marked signs, paved lanes, and maintained lines.

Often I would daydream, shift into autopilot, and shop. Wandering through stores while debriefing from a day of facts, figures, conference calls, arguments and demands, I'd gaze at shiny, beautiful, "on sale" display items. I'd lose myself in leather handbags and the beadwork on earrings. Freud or someone would tell you that my shopping and buying reflected my sublimated rage. Okay, so I did walk up to my share of perfume counters twitching and wild inside and not exactly in a floral mood.

At work, I felt helpless against the twin dragons of responsibility and productivity that consumed my time, my personal plans, my brain stamina, and any hope that I could keep my self original. So I cruised the stores like a zombie with a vengeance. Instead of pounding my fists on the hollow chest of a senior partner, I exploded in consumerism. A tasteful insanity that boosted the economy.

I remember the blue ceramic vase in this Olde English store thick with cranberry potpourri and Debussy, in tourist Georgetown. Priced to impress or depress, depending on your perspective. That night, I wanted to lord my well-paying job over the way-too-pleasant sales clerk with pimples and every happy person on earth, because I resented my workdays and had to have something to show for my misery. Like, perhaps, a vase.

This vase. I whipped out the credit card, my jaded partner in crime. "See how well she's doing," I heard guests whisper in my mind as they spied this *objet d'art* in my apartment and tittered appropriately among themselves. For an instant I warmed, and it almost felt like love. "I deserve a reward," I said to myself, my latest mantra of self-denial. I needed a bribe to endure my unbearable success.

But by the time the ceramic royalty had sat on my end table for a week, I decided it didn't match a single picture, table, chair, couch, lamp, or wall in the house. It sat aloof in its corner and became an animated, inanimate reproach. Okay, I'd wasted more money. My buying euphoria had settled into a now-familiar shame and private decadence. "Good thing I make a steep salary," I'd think to myself again, never noticing the link between my joyless job and my elevating expenses. The wrong career *creates* the need for money. Only the repressed turn reckless. The expressed have better things to do.

Face it. We live with ache until we live our dreams. Ache costs. We "reward" ourselves, distract ourselves, spoil ourselves, and survive ourselves, because we cannot bear to *feel* ourselves. An unlived dream will sit on your heart like a sumo wrestler. We can fail ourselves in silence, but not in ease or peace. This discomfort triggers us to search for lures, cures, drinks, parties, cruises, bungee jumping excursions, and good department stores. Substitutes for passion and fruition. Deprivation gnaws us to excess. Still, the need for a heartfelt life does not pass and the sumo wrestler does not budge or ever go on a diet.

> **The wrong career *creates* the need for money. Only the repressed turn reckless. The expressed have better things to do.**

Live your dream and you will live in balance. It's some kind of organic law of the universe. As your days become sweet, you will not seek distraction or relief. Your own creativity will fill the emptiness and still the pain; and it will also tickle you silly—and sane.

You will dance in your living room and on your terrace and sing to the moon and the hedges and the neighbor's cat, and the cat will even sing back. And you won't buy vases you don't need—or blouses or shoes or scarves or can openers.

We don't need "pick-me-ups" when our feet have left the ground and our hearts are laughing out loud. The right life is entrancing and sufficient unto itself.

My Future Or Now? The Investment Decision

"I remember saving this delicate bottle of French perfume.
I wouldn't let myself use it for just any old date or party.
It was the good stuff and I was saving it for the future.
Eventually, all that good stuff evaporated in the bottle."
A journal entry

"The only people who become wealthy by being concerned
with the future are insurance companies."
Leo Buscaglia

remember the first tax return I filled out after I'd left my high-salary career. Kir, my handholding friend, provided companionship and bracing of the soul as we sorted through regulations and official forms at a back booth at Village Inn. We drank recurring cups of coffee and scrawled in definitive numbers. Then I had to decide the big one. Should I tuck two thousand dollars away in an IRA as I had done in my responsible and respectable past that would make any banker proud? Or should I strut out on the edge and wing that money into the promise or the pandemonium of my freedom?

Spend retirement money? This would normally have occurred to me about as much as walking down the street in my stretch-marked birthday suit or singing the national anthem in a public library. For me, saving money for my future was like obeying the speed limit or using the proper salad fork in a red velvet restaurant. You just did it because it was the thing to do, and good, responsible citizen types told you to do it and it gave you a warm, cozy feeling as though you knew the rules in this world and so somehow you belonged.

I guess I also harbored some subconscious superstition that if I had money in the bank, nothing too atrocious could happen to me, or at least nothing that I couldn't write a designer check for. It never occurred to me that adamantly saving for my future might in itself rob me of the future I supposed would come.

But this transcendental career change sometimes felt like waking up in a Peter Max poster where suddenly every assumption I'd ever made turned lime green and seemed obscene. Working at the law firm, I could afford to tuck two thousand dollars into a cookie jar on the back shelf and not even miss a ski trip or a beat in my shopping sprees.

But now I was living one of those "out there," front shelf kind of lives. No longer generating a casual and comfortable income, I had to reconsider if it was really responsible to deprive myself of money I could invest in *today's* dreams so that maybe later, if I lived that long, I could enjoy "leisure" in Miami Beach. At this turning point in my life, every decision seemed to demand the upstream faith of a mad, pre-spawning salmon. So could I really afford to be as mincing with my resources as my great, great grandmothers who hid their pennies under the bed, and passed on this lineage of holding back and making due with lack? Salmon or grandmothers? And was spending my IRA money self-investment or the handiwork of its greasy, fast-talking cousin, self-indulgence?

The IRA decision raised a question I would have to answer again and again on this path: My future or now? Where would I bet my strength? What part of my life did I want to secure? Where would I plunk down the actual currency of my conviction? My future or now?

Up until this point in my life I had practically become an Olympic athlete in the little known sport of delayed gratification. Oh sure, I had my shopping sprees and commercial excesses, but in the big, big things, I had always denied myself today's longing for the sake of tomorrow's gold medal, gold watch, and golden years. Working

> There might not have been a future for me to grow old in, if I hadn't grown young and wild in that moment.

myself to death, I told myself, someday I will have enough security to relax. Someday all my exhaustion and self-denial will pay off. Someday I will know the good life and, of course, I won't be too pissed off, chronically fatigued, toxic, or out of touch with myself to enjoy it. Someday, but not today.

Finally my tomorrow worship came to an end. After stuffing down my deepest desires for so long, my emotional pipeline had clogged. The raw sewage of depression backed up on me. Suddenly, I couldn't will myself to be patient one second more for relief that would come later.

In fact, I could barely will myself to keep breathing, stay focused, and avoid doing something really dumb and irrevocable. Maybe you've known such an out-of-control time. But by the time I started having daily fantasies about the bus I took to work crashing or detonating so I wouldn't have to go in (but I wouldn't have to quit either), I knew I needed freedom, even recklessness, more than caution. That's why I finally took time off to fly to California, lie on the beach, dare the indecency of life outside my box, and dream about becoming a writer, a seashell collector, and a sunset watcher extraordinaire.

In the back booth of Village Inn, I recalled the wild green waves of the Pacific Ocean, the stinging cold water that broke through the cloying layers of my depression. I remembered how only the salt and the sting of *the present* had brought me to life, revived me when all my money in the bank and iron-clad tomorrows had failed me with their meaninglessness and intangibility. No dividend could rekindle or comfort my wailing soul. But life in its libertine grandeur could. The ocean did. My freedom anchored me in a way that all the "guarantees" of tomorrow's creature comforts could not. There might not have been a future for me to grow old in, if I hadn't grown young and wild in that moment.

That evening at Village Inn, I permanently revised my understanding of foresight. I no longer believed I could ensure a safe tomorrow by sacrificing the dreams of today. Instead, I would feed myself the minerals and nutrients of the day before me rather than starve myself in the hopes of attending a posh banquet down the road. Only through nurturing today's strength could I create a today *and* a tomorrow that would sustain me in all ways.

Please don't hear me as saying you should never save money for the future. All I am saying is I wouldn't suggest saving money for your future at the cost of your present soul survival. You don't have to get reckless, but you might have to get extraordinary. This career transition is an exotic time in your life with just plain out-of-the-ordinary guidelines and dispensations.

Deductions for IRA? That night I wrote zero. I had two thousand dollars more for the exact moment in which I stood, the starting gate for the race of a lifetime. I had two thousand dollars more to explore myself, learn new ways to work, enroll in classes, take healing trips to the mineral springs in New Mexico, and pay for private counseling and the re-grouting of those grooves in my brain, not to mention buy groceries and car insurance.

And best of all, I knew I *was* saving for my future. I was saving myself.

"So, What Do I Love to Do?"
You Ask and Ask and Ask

*ow some of you will receive a Western Union from God as to your "burning mission," but you're probably the same type of people who win Lotto and vacations on the radio. Meanwhile, the rest of us will beat ourselves up thinking that we're really supposed to have the skies crack open and a ticker-tape parade march down the main street of our hearts. Finally, fear will tell you your inner bleariness is **the** sign that you really don't have a creative purpose and should just stop flattering yourself with faith, hope, and other extravagances.*

*But the truth is, you will stumble into clarity. Actually, you will finally run smack into a sense of self-permission, then admission. **You see, you already know what you'd die to do.** You just keep ignoring that temptation that makes you giggle and flush in hopes that you can find a smugly sensible resolution instead.*

Ah, but you are about to discover a radical new kind of sensibility.

Ushering In The Exiled Love

"Be patient toward all that is unsolved in your heart
and try to love the questions themselves."
Rainer Maria Rilke

⌐◦⌐

"The shifting voices of a thousand selves eventually must tire and
dwindle. One voiceless voice dwells in the void and discerns.
Wait and you shall have the knowledge you seek.
Rush and your own anxiety will answer you."
A journal entry

I sat at a Popeye's Famous Fried Chicken staring at a red plastic cup filled with pink lemonade. The cup read "Love That Chicken. Popeye's." Its clarity jabbed at me. I wondered what *I* loved.

My life loomed before me as wide open as a prairie. I could choose to study nuclear physics or metaphysics, sling nachos in a ski town, crank out briefs for the district attorney, or buy a van and drive to Baja or Wichita or anywhere. Popeye's—the great vortex for major decisions. Choices whipped through my mind like socks and bras in the dryer. "The heart knows the way," I told myself quietly. "The mind stammers with ramifications and complications. But the heart knows. The heart knows."

Still, a caged panther paced in my journal. I found myself scrawling, "Sitting at the edge of the universe. Sitting at the fork in the road, the whole damn flatware set. I am drinking lemonade and I am starkly conscious of each sip just as I am now aware that I am about to choose my whole life. How will I know my direction? How will I know what to choose?" And again, my mantra calmed me, "The heart knows. The heart knows. There's nothing to choose. Just something to set loose."

Just something to set loose. A desire I already had, but I continued to refuse. And it's true. Most of us will look right past the shooting stars coming out of left field. We want answers that seem real. Sure we want direction that will revolutionize our living and rouse a chorus in our thinning bones. But we don't want to wander past the gates of the estate and step into the ozone. That's okay, though. Because with resistance and close-mindedness comes emptiness and frustration. Frustration will do the job quite nicely. Frustration pressures mountains into volcanoes and "confusion" into unconditional honesty and acceptance. And that's all you need.

For example, despite my insistent claims that I had no idea what I wanted to do for a living, deep down I'd known for years that I wanted to write. But I thought that maybe if I ignored *this* mad preference, I'd come up with a more palatable option like macroeconomics or cardiovascular surgery. Writing poetry seemed to me more like a strange road trip than an actual livelihood. I was looking for solutions, not further detours into the fringes of reality.

"I have no idea what I want to do," I'd stomp and storm in therapy. "I thought you mentioned that you'd like to write," interjected the well-paid neutral professional, smoothing his neutral tie and tone of voice. "Yeah, but I can't do *that*!" I insisted as visions of an unwashed self starving in the gutter rushed to mind, followed by the image of my very Republican father glowering at me as though I had told him "Daddy, I'm going to be a poet and shoot up on metaphors and take to the streets in tie-dyed robes and bare feet." So, week after week in that safe beige office, I'd lie to myself, deny myself out loud. "I don't know what I want to do. I have no idea what I want to do."

Many conversations, dollars, journal writings, and visits to the Popeye's on my corner later, my yearning had not changed. But desperation finally drove my mind into forbidden possibilities. Because I couldn't bear to remain locked outside myself anymore, I had become available even to the unforgivable. "I want to write," I heard myself say one day in a hoarse and hopeful voice. And with that fatal and glorious admission, all the doors swung open and my questions lit away like startled pigeons. I was left in daylight with the most obvious answer possible. I could no longer remain

The heart speaks with closure to the open mind.

within the comfort zone of the search. There was nothing left to find. The heart speaks with closure to the open mind.

So ease up on your skirmish for clarity. The vagueness will clear when you decide to embrace *whatever* you hear. I like to remember that I don't have to struggle for what I already possess. You came with instincts and imperatives, and they will thrust through the mud and bud in their own glad season. It's not your answers or ideas that you need to worry about. It's your *resistance* to your ideas, any immediate reaction to choke the strange and uncomfortable. Take care of these weeds and the creative seeds will take care of themselves.

There's nothing to choose. Just something to set loose. Meanwhile, relax and receive. Receive and believe. The heart *always* knows. You have everything you need.

You May Have To Color Outside
The Lines To Find Your Picture

"I've noticed that my 'acceptable' self mocks, trivializes,
and thwarts my truth-seeking process in any way it can;
the captain of the ship abhors mutiny."
A journal entry

~

"Be not the slave of your own past—plunge into the sublime seas,
dive deep, and swim far, so you shall come back with
self-respect, with new power, with an advanced experience,
that shall explain and overlook the old."
Ralph Waldo Emerson

*M*ost career questionnaires, checklists, and even personality type classifications would only promise me a context in a world of limits. Traditional inquiries had traditional ends in mind. I needed to birth constellations, galaxies, an uncharted and impossible lifestyle, and a few poems here and there. Of course, I suffered through the routine investigations first, hoping for fireworks and revelations. I searched for the unlimited in the delineated. Like looking in the zoo for panthers in the wild.

Just when I felt pent up with destiny, but tangled in "reality," Kir, unconventional counselor and blessed friend, offered strange assistance. He dared and prodded me with dreamwork, writing assignments involving "The Warden Within" or "The Oracle Within" and question grenades like "What would you do just for the joy of it on the last day of your life?" I'd roll my eyes and frown my offense, but eventually I'd crouch down in the mental sandbox and play with him.

My rational mind slipped on a banana peel every time Kir asked a "silly" question. Meanwhile, he coaxed my child mind to drop clues, golden wish by golden wish, to the long lost castle of my heart. Kir reminded me that underneath the blazing, barren sands of my conscious mind's frustration, a river of truth teemed. Just because I didn't have the words yet—didn't mean I didn't have the answers.

I furrowed my brow when Kir set a package of doodle markers on the table at the Village Inn diner. They winked beside the copper pitcher of coffee. "Draw me a picture of how you feel right now," he nudged.

For weeks I'd been languishing in currents of emotions I could not tame, name, or reason away. I felt lost inside myself without a flashlight or a flare. Still, my "I'm a Harvard lawyer" self prickled at the idea of fooling with colored pens, especially in public, and worst of all at bright-eyed, long-haired Kir's command.

"What?" I said, indignation glaring in my voice. My eyes stabbed at the package of pinks, oranges, yellows, and blues. I peered around me at the families eating their mashed potatoes and grilled cheese sandwiches, parents talking about their bosses, their kids, their mashed potatoes, and grilled-cheese sandwiches. No one was splitting their psyches with loose-leaf paper and felt tip pens. "I'm an attorney, not a twelve-year-old," I barked at Kir, shoving away the fat, bright markers and arching my back against the green vinyl booth. What if someone should see me? One of the word processors at the firm, the president of the bar association, a client, or a cameraman from the evening news? "Coming up this hour, Harvard lawyer doodles during the dinner hour at Village Inn." I could feel my stomach muscles tensing.

"I can't do this," I insisted.

"Go ahead, just play," Kir baited. "You may think you're so drop-dead important, but are you happy?" He slid the package of markers over to my side of the table along with a clean sheet of paper. "Draw a design of what your life feels like right now." He gently touched my hand. Tears boiled within. My life felt crazy and so did I. I so wanted those impossible answers.

Quick glance over each padded shoulder: people chewing, wiping children's chins, slurping strawfuls of Coca Cola, wielding forks and knives and details of the day, no one looking our way. I selected a sky blue marker and bit off the cap. "What should I draw?" I asked.

"Doesn't matter. Just draw what your life feels like right now." Within seconds, the pens seemed to know what to do. Lines and colors and stars erupted before me. I raged upon the page until I felt emptied and quieted inside. Finished, my drawing swirled with striped roads and brick roads and a profusion of paths of other distinct patterns.

The drawing blurted out my confusion, my overwhelming sense of choice. A wide path of stars and bright colors also mirrored the wee and secret celebration that a part of me felt. I knew that path was the path of creative writing, and it stood out from all the others. The emotional clarity and candor of the communication amazed me.

You won't find the secret notes to a saxophone life with a bookkeeping mind.

Thrilled me. *Connected* me. My blues and pinks and dots and stars revealed more than I could ever say.

At last, I felt the seeping peace of self-realization. I had begun a different kind of exploration to find a different kind of work and life. And it had worked. I would never find the summation of my life in labels, charts, or cookie-cutter job descriptions. *My creative calling would only answer a creative inquiry.* This kind of inquiry demanded an intimate relationship with myself. Only when I could feel my feelings in the moment could I discern the felt-sense of the direction that called me now.

Kir smiled. So did I. I didn't care if anyone at the Village Inn saw me with Crayola markers doodling my way to pink and purple freedom. You won't either. Draw. Meditate. Journal. Walk on the beach or daydream with a supportive confidante. Befriend your soul. Let your big and deep instincts have big and deep breathing room.

Open the blinds. You won't find the secret notes to a saxophone life with a bookkeeping mind. If you want to discover an unimaginable livelihood, you just might have to leave standardized inquiries behind.

Drop The Gun And Have Some Fun

"Freedom inspires freedom."
A journal entry

---

*"The creation of something new is not accomplished by the intellect
but by the play instinct acting from inner necessity."*
C. G. Jung

O n my designated Sunday, among browsers and buyers, I ogled the creative writing corner at The Tattered Cover bookstore. Provocative designs, titles, shelves of spines like racks of fine wines. My stomach tittered with an exotic nervousness. I'd promised myself that day I would buy a how-to creative writing book. Backed by self-permission, I had come on this crucial mission. *I was here to feed my joy.*

Some dreamer, writer, creative wannabe within me had been starving for decades. And, at last, here I stood before a spread of soul nourishment. I eyed the desserts, the pastries and pies, each book that promised a sugar-high of writing euphoria. Part of me skipped and whooped inside, eyes wide, to see the purchase "we" would bring home and devour. The adult part of me scrutinized titles and scanned the contents, narrowing choices and wading through promises.

After a very quick hour, I'd sampled too many books and my mind buzzed with just a little too much hope and wonder. Long ago I'd whizzed through Europe and feasted on so many fabled cathedrals and pigeon-infested piazzas that, one day, I just curled up in the tour bus, refused to see even one more sight, and plunged into an American romance novel instead. Now, like then, I could stand no more invigoration. Positioning my tentative armload of books back on their shelves, I scrambled for my car keys, mentally murmured "another time," and proceeded to stumble out of the store.

Yet on impulse, stronger and quicker than any conscious thought could direct me, I spun around. I marched over to the shelves of promise and seized the first book that had captivated me an hour before, *Writing the Natural Way* by Gabrielle Rico. On blunt instinct, I knew the book to grab, the one that had grabbed me. Then as suddenly, I bolted toward the cashier.

"Fast. Fast. Fast," I thought, "before I change my mind, get 'reasonable,' or all murky with guilt."

"That all?" asked the dark-haired clerk with oversized glasses as she held up the book. "Yes," I replied in a quick, sharp, I-mean-business tone, aiming to convince myself I really did mean business and would not slink around, put the book back, turn into a lawyer again as the clock struck high noon, and undermine my dreams right then and there.

I think I know now how bank robbers feel as they wait for tellers to stuff their bounty into a satchel. I held my breath as I watched the clerk slip the book and receipt in the thin brown bag. I stared at her hands, the turquoise ring on her finger, the criss-cross lines on her knuckles. I swear the clocks slowed down in that moment. I felt dizzy and lucid all at the same time. In that singular action, I knew I was reversing my history: *accepting and supporting my creativity.* The love imprisoned in me was breaking free from dictatorship and ancient captivity. Tears stung my eyes.

I practically giggled as she handed me the bag, validated my parking garage stub, smiled, and raised her eyes to the next customer, just like that. Clutching my toy to my chest, I shoved through the crowd and hustled toward the exit. Wow, would I get away with it? Slip a creative writing book past my mean-spirited internal censor? Would I finally ignore that sour-breathed advisor who had always banished enthusiasm with its sick idea of realism, pointing fingers and thundering, "This will go nowhere. This is a waste of time that will cost you. This is PLAY."

For years, this inner critical voice had fancied itself "reasonable" and concerned for my welfare. For "my own good," it trivialized my dreams and desires, and stomped out sparks and fires. This part of myself viewed times of enchantment as lapses of indulgence sure to lead to ruin and blight, flying without a kite, and forgetting to balance my checkbook and my life. And accordingly, I had always tried to keep an eye on myself, clip my own buds and wings, put paperweights on my longings, and perform like a good little heavy-hearted girl.

Yet this time, the child in me had acted fast, backed by the extravagant commitment I'd made before I'd left the house: *"Today, I explore my interests with attention, not condemnation."* For too long I'd listened to the joyless voice of the joyless way. That's why I still didn't know what I *wanted* to do with my life. I only knew what I definitely *didn't* want to do.

I'd listened to my head long enough. I bought the book even though I didn't know why other than it made my heart chirp and I was listening for chirping these days. And a good thing too. Because that first creative writing book prompted taking writing classes, buying other books, and eventually writing my own book and teaching my own classes. I never could have figured out this path. *I just had to let it out.* That's all we will ever do. But the real work comes in abandoning the notion of work and plans and big important questions answered—and trusting fun instead.

Our fun is more than fun; it's the vortex and hot spot of uncanny wisdom.

It's the unencumbered mind or child self that retains our joy and the connection to things unseen, but known. It's our first nature that knows the code of our bones. I always tell my students that our fun is more than fun; it's the vortex and hot spot of uncanny wisdom. Our canned wisdom—our judgments, fore-casts, and "realism"—corrupt these original responses and twin-kling inklings.

Welcome bursts of impudence. Don't sabotage yourself with "prudence." It goes beyond saying, but I'll say it anyway: If you want to find work that feels like play, you do have to play. *You do have to play.*

Take your young heart to the toy store and have a look around. Call it research and development. Ah, first question. What is the toy store for you? A wellness or nutrition center? A computer chain? A crafts and hobby shop? Or maybe a trail in the mountains where wild rose grows? I'm not advocating wanton materialism. I am suggesting you investigate and feed your interests. Exploration will inform, invigorate, embolden you, and take hold of you.

Dabble on the wild side. Rummage through your child side. Let wonder and innocence take you to the park to try on the shiny new roller skates of instinct. Something in you knows how to glide. It doesn't come with planning or foresight or lots of furrows on your brow. It comes with a squeal and a direction for now.

Only The Real Dream Has The Power

*" 'I see this character in a purple sharkskin suit,' you suddenly
think, and then the voice of the worried mother says,
'No, no put him in something respectable.' "*
Anne Lamott

~

"Go beyond reason to Love. It is safe. It is the only safety."
T. Golas

Yes, welcome that intoxicating and abominable interest, the
one you shudder to admit to yourself. The one that transports
your heart, assails your brain, and freaks your mother into paying
half your therapy bill and possibly some of her own. The most
practical thing you can do is ignore practicality. You have fero-
cious magic at your disposal, but magic only favors dizzy inspiration. Caution and control do not draw on the spell.

Choose gloriously. Seize your wild want, not that freeze-
dried, politically correct, mild want. Thinned-down desires douse
the fire. If you choose some version of your dream you could "settle for," the substitute won't lure you to swim the oceans, scrape up
the mountains, or cross deserts in the summertime with just a
Twinkie in your pocket, crooning with gratitude. Only the real
dream has the power.

When I shelved law to write professionally, I plotted to temper and "practicalize" my inspired path. I buckled down to write magazine articles instead of skipping with my pen to the riverbanks and poppy fields of imagination. I figured it was more reasonable to choose journalism, saleable writing, over up-in-the-air, sallying-on-sunbeams, creative writing. And so came my downfall. Because my strategy was reasonable, not extravagantly divine.

Writing articles, packaging stories into word lengths and agreeable perspectives, kept my feet on the ground and the golden stallions of my creativity stalled out in their stalls. Without wild want, I lacked the will to endure form rejection letters, late and low payments, the frostbite of frustrated editors, and those practical assignments like writing about "how to make holiday candles from excess earwax." While I sold some pieces, I did not have the energy to keep pitching stories to magazines and stories to myself about how this was really okay because it was sort of like

> Choose gloriously. Seize your wild want, not that freeze-dried, politically correct, mild want.

creative writing and I was sort of living my dreams. It's just that I sort of preferred to stare into space and reread the pizza ads in my junk mail. I would have dragged through the desert licking Twinkie wrappers, but not for an "almost" dream. Only the real one has the power.

⌢

When I finally allowed myself to write poetry, short stories, and the essays that would become this book, I experienced the power of devotion. Now I understand how ancient Egyptians hauled bricks in the middle of a desert to raise their pyramids, or how parents work second jobs to buy their young ones shiny lunch boxes and higher educations. Once you taste love, you taste power. Something kicks in that says *whatever it takes, whatever it takes.* You've crossed to the other side.

I know that once I stopped trying to fit what I wanted to do into some kind of real-world form, what I wanted to do sprouted urgent feathers and took flight. I didn't care where it led because I could never go back to a life of limits on my love. I know it sounds preposterous to choose something when you can't imagine how it could work. But on this path, it's riskier to see how it can work and how it will taint your love. Choose the storm instead of the form.

Desire will take you beyond every limitation. *Unless you limit your desire.* How much do you burn to do the work you love? Will you let yourself want this want with all your heart? Or will you hold back a ripple of enthusiasm to "protect" yourself?

What we hold back, holds *us* back. It's too easy to quit when we don't really want the prize. Weak tea doesn't warm the bones like the brandy of desire, and soon a bitter cold can send us running for cover. It takes more than reasonable plans to unleash unreasonable strength.

Submit to your heart's most wondrous desire, even while you do not know how to translate this delicious nuisance into a career that buys Purina for your cat, Cheerios for your children, and that paper with the want ads—just in case. Feed your want. It is your strength and the source of a rollicking creativity. You can move mountains if you are moved.

I invite you to move a mountain or two. Set your fury free. Favor your sublime, assigned desire, the only one that chills, thrills, and stills you.

You will find magic in the madness—and nowhere else.

How To Skip Through Fog

"It seems like guidance is a lot like candlelight.
It lights up a room or a moment at a time.
I can see where I am right now. I can't see where I'm going.
But I bring this flicker with me as I step forward."
A journal entry

⁓

"My heart guides me tenderly and truly. I find ways
through the wilderness. My heart finds paths through the desert."
Julia Cameron

I remember walking in the mountains during a wet and white fog, my dirt road enmeshed in fallen clouds. Amid this mysterious landscape, the ground beneath my feet and the scenery at my side emerged crystal clear, enunciated, and alive. The dark green needles on the branch of a pine tree silently hosted pinpoints and globules of rain. I could see the rainbow in each prism of moisture. And beside my thick rubber boots, the yellow of a small wildflower shouted its presence from between freckled pebbles and the memory of a tire groove.

When I strained to see down the road, even a few feet ahead, I could not. As much as my immediate surroundings emerged in crisp and glistening focus, the yonder blurred. I could not glimpse my future path, but I could walk step by obvious step home. Just like my life, I thought.

I know of no other way to find and follow your calling than to take the next visible step before you. Clients come to me hoping for maps, Triple A "TripTiks" and other itineraries, and I tell them they must enter the shadows of their mythical forest and stalk their infallible breadcrumbs. A crust of rye or wheat sings to the instinct one footstep at a time. Some direction or action twinkles and hums more than another, even if just by a whisper or an extra goose bump. The present moment does not lack clarity. Quick, move before the crows steal your impression.

I look back at the trail of breadcrumbs I've followed with fascination, mirth, and a hearty salute to the unpredictable and incomprehensible. Basically, I left law to write poems and unravel the mystery of myself. While writing poetry, I decided to write a non-fiction book to put my message out into the world and to carve my word sculptures into prose. Work on the book spilled into offering support groups in my living room, then workshops and retreats, then coaching private clients. Radio shows. Interviews. Travel and speaking engagements. Meanwhile, the adventure romps on.

Yet I never consciously set out to do any of this. Not any of it. And thank goodness for the foresight to have no foresight because I could never have mapped out this unthinkable tapestry of grace. "Where can writing poetry ever take me in life?" I groaned and wailed in journals and in coffeehouses to nodding and wide-eyed friends. So glad I wrote poems and found out.

"But, but, but," we all say. We want a plan, a program, a blueprint. We want a double-decker bus, a schedule, and a campy tour guide. We want order, control, and a telescope into the future, not some firm and feel-good step on a mushy, murky route into bewilderment. We demand a static definition for this ecstatic evolution. That's nice. But no dice. It's just one foot in front of the other on a road your intellect may never understand, and your heart will never doubt. The path of inspiration defies navigation. We arrive by way of revelation.

With this breath, you know a present action to take, a place to start. Sure, it looks foggy up ahead, and it probably always will on this fabulous and frustrating road. But this present action will feed you soul and certainty like a bowl of barley soup on a winter's day. Then you will know your next step, just as you know the direction to attempt right now. Go ahead. Step into the glory. You will find your way by going deep into the inklings you find. Trust me. *Trust you.* And have a nice trip.

> The path of inspiration defies navigation.
> We arrive by way of revelation.

Transition Blues and Tender Greens

Chapter Five

*O*kay, I hate to break it to you, but get ready for maddening days. You've just leaped from an established life and you're all gung ho—crazed really—to begin a new established life and yet, what's this, you suddenly can't heave yourself out of bed and it takes you eight hours to finish your "morning" coffee. All your spitfire has fizzled and you're moving in slow motion and now you've started to scare yourself into thinking that maybe this is it: You really are incompetent and you've just started your brand new futile life.

Well, please stop terrorizing yourself. You're right on track. I know you want to do, do, do. But this time asks of you your "undoing." Floating without a context or a business card. Unleashing tears you may have shunned for years. Dying to your shell and inhabiting life with sudden sensitivity. Yes, you will kick up every value, belief, hope, and doubt. But what settles down creates your new, solid ground.

The Year Of Sleeping Dangerously

⌒

*T*wo minutes after you make your grand entrance into a bold new life, don't be surprised if passion and anticipation give way to a divine sludge. It's like the second you fly the coop, you land in this vat of emotional pea soup. Now home and alone, litheness slows to listlessness, a maddening drop in energy. Should this happen to you, know that you are not crazy or alone. You have just entered the transition zone. Congratulations. Collapse is progress.

After I walked out of my high-paced, breathless career, I functioned at what seemed to be two notches above the living dead line. I waited tables, bought groceries, and fed my cat. But I slept for what seemed to be unnatural numbers of hours. My mind revved up like an eager sports car engine racing with the need to create a new and improved life. But I found my physical self dragging around the apartment in slow motion in my underwear in the middle of the day, then taking naps to recuperate. I felt like a beached whale hungering for the sea. I ate bagels and cream cheese and leftovers and lunchmeats instead. Guilt took finky little notes about my attraction to the refrigerator and shared them hourly.

It didn't take long before I found myself haunted by rattling questions and rude images of wasting away in oblivion while the rest of the world drank lattés to go. Would I just exist in limbo now? Was gazing at my walls for hours "following my bliss?" Just how much could I eat anyway? And how would I pursue "the hero's journey" if it took me three hours to get up and brush my teeth? "Oh, this is great," I thought, "I've wrecked a Rolls-Royce career so that I can grow as wide as a Buddha and contemplate the daisies on my quilt."

> "Oh, this is great," I thought, "I've wrecked a Rolls-Royce career so that I can grow as wide as a Buddha and contemplate the daisies on my quilt."

This is what I think now. I think we experience a form of higher-powered paralysis to protect us from getting in our own clever way. I think most of us would skip soul searching and start job searching and that is not the purpose of this time out of ordinary time. You did not leave a job to find a job, but to find yourself, the queen you locked away, while you served lesser things and others' kings. So in this slow-down, melt-down phase of your journey, you have the opportunity to sort through the layers of your self and decide which ones travel on and which ones get shelved. The fire we seek will burn through old roles. We will lose our well-told stories to find our whispering soul.

I slept because I mourned the death or loss of an identity. My Leaning Tower of Pisa had finally crashed. And while I wanted to be positive and enthusiastic and all that, all I could see was dust and ash. Then, too, I slept because the process of excavating the real me out of the rubble required emotional devotion and concentration. Each week when I trudged to therapy, I'd learn more about that creative little girl whose dreams hadn't fit the dreams of an emphatic and pragmatic family. Surprisingly, her tears of alienation still waited within me. They had waited while I marched off to law school and then worked a maniacal career and said, "Not now dear, not now."

Well, now had come with a drum roll, a violin, a toll, and a vengeance. The world doesn't approve when we cry. Pain embarrasses our efficient society. So I hid in bed, my own private retreat center in the middle of the city. I had my cat for on-call healing sessions and I burned rain-scented incense and candles. It wasn't quite an executive spa, but I figured it was better than an institution.

But every moment I "rested," I never felt more restless. I yearned to plunge into another career, a definition, live my life's purpose, turn into an Action Jackson, and assume my place in the busy, dizzy world I saw outside my window. I hadn't wanted to just leave something, but to leave *for* something. But the "something" remained mysterious. I could not pierce the veil. I could barely read the mail. When friends or family called and asked, "What are you doing these days?" I didn't have the insight to know I was *undoing*.

This undoing process works like painting the interior of an old house. First, you clean the walls, sand them down, and patch them up, or else you paint over the old infirmities, the same warps and clumps of history. If I'd run out and grabbed another career without delving into where I had betrayed myself the first time, I'd have ended up with a new color of wet paint over the same pattern of bumps and desperately limited opinions about myself, my dreams, and my reality. So as much as I wanted to get started on a new career, all I could do was get started on a new philosophy or mythology of who I was and who I was to be.

In retrospect I can tell you that the "doing" of our chosen work comes easy. It is this time of "undoing" that requires every ounce of strength, vision, and persistence. It is meeting the dream-slashing and faith-bashing denouncer, and journaling, praying, and processing your way back to your true-heartedness, the part of you that dreams your dream and knows the shortest path to the quickest stream. Every belief that ever held you back from your desires will now come forth and stand before your door. This time will make you stand in your strength like you never have before.

You might think this psychic showdown slows you down. But that's because, in the old way of doing things that created lives we did not want, we insisted that actions furthered us more than feeling our way through healing. But on this inside-out, inspired path to true work, the relationship we develop with ourselves is more important than anything else. There is nothing else. All work we love comes from the love we give ourselves.

Months down the road, my grieving and self-exploration gave way to curiosity and wonder. The naps with a life-force of their own ended. Stabs at creativity and expression began. The juice returned and the breath-stealing adventure before me unfurled its shapely red cape. I have almost never felt as small or lost since.

Today I speak in front of crowds of people, but that doesn't take near as much fortitude as undoing an intact identity, deciding to die midstream to a life you've always known. I know who the real hero is. I owe every triumph I experience to a tender part of myself who, years ago, got under flowered quilts, yawned, and surrendered to a process that didn't look like progress. It took that kind of inner revolution, maddening and frightening, for me to discover a unified self that moved with love and prowess.

You No Longer Have A Label,
But You Do Have A Ticket

"Nameless: the origin of heaven and earth."
Tao Te Ching

~

"I'm beginning to feel like I've returned a sweater that didn't quite
fit right to the great big customer service department in the sky.
I've got my money back, all in crisp new bills, and I'm off to
this fair where all the primo merchants are already arranging
their wares. I can smell the cotton candy in the air.
I have another chance now."
A journal entry

When I first dropped out of my lawyer life, I sometimes walked downtown on weekdays like some wayward ghost haunting a former territory. I'd stare at the office high-rises with fountains gushing in plazas, and geometric murals in cool lobbies. Then I'd gaze in the windows of trendy boutiques dangling smart black leather bags, silk shirts, tweed blazers, the fashion of validity. I found myself envious of the women, like the woman I used to be, who could sit at outdoor cafés sipping iced tea in the easy security of a crowd just like them. They ate Cobb salads, wore linen suits, and consulted their bulky daytimers just bulging with appointments. After lunch, they rushed back to meetings, matters, and materiality, smart black leather bags by their side.

Meanwhile, I walked, invisible, past sidewalk vendors and lawyers, accountants and secretaries in line for automated bank machines. After lunch hour, the streets would begin to thin out, the remains of life still tingling in the air. I'd find myself missing what I hated, only because that bustle and busyness felt substantial and I did not. I didn't want to practice law. And I didn't want to return to the sleek oppression of an office on the thirtieth floor. Yet I longed for the coherence of a world. I wanted places to go and hats to wear and the easy well-being of knowing just where I belonged. Dangling on the sidelines, I longed for a part in the play.

Just months before, I'd had a business card, letterhead, people who recognized me in the mirrored elevator, and a set of circumstances that met with immediate acceptability instead of eyebrows raised, throats cleared, and, usually, poor advice offered. In contrast, my new transition status attracted interrogations, opinions, advice, jealousy, distaste, and lots of face-scrunching, strained looks. I so wished I'd had a word or term that could have passed for an identity. "I'm a creative entrepreneur, an explorer, a dabbler." I would have given anything for a pigeonhole to hide in instead of parading my great, big, wide-open soul—or this silent, default characterization: "I'm a screw up." "I'm a lost soul."

For example, I remember standing around at a former colleague's baby shower, of course in her newly remodeled, gawk-worthy home with her happy, rich husband and all their well-appointed friends. Like always, the inevitable nightmare question came up, either as, "So what are you doing now?" or "What do you do for a living?" My face would turn plum and my fingers would strum my sweater as I'd aim for some slick reply and end up sounding like a flower child gone to seed. There I'd go, babbling about Buddhism's theory of right livelihood,

I came to the realization that, while I no longer had a label, I did have a ticket, a ticket to anywhere I wanted to go with my life.

how Joseph Campbell trusted the universe, how this society just didn't get artists and visionaries, and what my therapist thought of me and my relationship to my critical father figure this week. Just a little more than anyone at a baby shower ever wanted to know.

Conversations about careers often degenerated that way. The more I tried to convince someone how sane and evolved I was, or how safe and loving my journey, the more we both felt like I was flying in a balloon created from chicken feathers and finger paint. My free-flowing, see-what-happens career plan all made so much sense until I offered it in defense. Then the psychic glue came undone and so did my tongue. Everyone stared at the bean dip.

So I learned the hard way, the embarrassing, painful, sheepish way, to shut up, eat more olives, stop going to parties, and stop trying to explain an inexplicable, soul-filled odyssey in an eat-some-peanuts-and-have-some-small-talk kind of way. At this amazing point in my life, I did not have an identity or role. I had a gap in my life that was just plain off the map, and it actually felt better when I didn't try to cover it up like a great big stain on the rug. It was there. I was there. And I was definitely out there, in process land, the territory between safe places.

Many of us don't seem to know what to do with ourselves when we're in process. It's almost like we see process as failure instead of promise. It will be like this for you, perhaps. It's as if everyone else out there is walking around like a finished product while, in the meantime, our Jell-O hasn't jelled, and we haven't even found one of those tinny molds of a dolphin or a rose to hold us. But that's okay because Jell-O without a mold is Jell-O genesis that can become absolutely any Jell-O creation it wants to be.

And gradually process became a good thing, a desirable thing, even an enviable position. Because I came to the realization that, while I no longer had a label, I did have a ticket, a ticket to anywhere I wanted to go with my life. I didn't just have a blank hole on my résumé. I had a blank canvas. I could say yes to any desire, dance partner, sunbeam, hope, heartthrob, divine invitation, or adventure that crossed my path. *Something would come.* And meanwhile, I stood in an open field with all the stars above my head and my brazen arms wide open, unconditional. I knew I stood in exactly the right place where magic could find me. My vulnerability was the secret to my flexibility, and flexibility meant that I could move like tumbleweed on the wings of a heaven-sent wind. That wind would blow. And at the same time, I stood stripped of former commitments, poised to flow.

So it's up to you how you see this time. You are either on the verge of an adventure that will lead to gleaming paths materializing beneath your feet, or you're lost and just too creaking old for this kind of precariousness and uncertainty. You can tingle with anticipation or anxiety. Either way, you're probably in for some tingling, some reshaping of your energy. If you choose to embrace your process instead of fight it, it's less likely to throw you from one side of the room to the other.

Trade in that label for a ticket. One explains you properly and makes you a perfectly conventional guest at a cocktail party; the other is the price of admission to a dance of no regret and no turning back. Sure, the place between places is awkward and different and people may look at you funny. But freedom always enters ordinary rooms flaunting exotic robes.

These days, I'll take inspiration over definition any day of the week. And someday soon, I will find the nerve to answer, "What do you do for a living?" with the simple reply, "I live."

Maybe you will, too.

First We Turn Red, Then True Blue

*"To be ourselves causes us to be exiled by many others, and yet
to comply with what others want causes us to be exiled from ourselves."*
Clarissa Pinkola Estés

~

*"When we finish convincing ourselves, we finish shouting.
We keep the message, but adjust the volume.
Proclamation mellows into a lifestyle."*
A journal entry

*B*eginning to live your life out loud, a life you've always dreamed of but one you've also shunned, will feel delicious and strange. You may go through some versions of yourself before you hit your authentic range. For a decade of my life, the creative or artistic part of myself had never said, "this is me." If anything, I went way out of my way to prove that I could slay dragons, balance checkbooks, disavow my sensitivity, and be as clipped and corporate as they come. So when my creative self finally slipped out of the darkness, she emerged in leopard skins and lime green flip-flops, igniting Roman candles and shouting ARTIST from the rooftops. Transition times have us daring wondrous and uncomfortable things. We will bumble and bruise ourselves, stumble and peruse ourselves. It's just that we have to test our voices before we know the notes to sing.

I remember buying a black cape of a coat and a brimming black hat with a billowing, striped feather at a thrift store. Outlandish. Swaggering. Sublime. Artistic. Perfect for Denver's Capitol Hill neighborhood, which reminded me of New York's Greenwich Village where it seemed like all the free-spirited, poetry-loving souls lived and smoked clove cigarettes. I swirled in the mirror, posed and postured, and granted exclusive interviews to my feature-writing cat, signed imaginary bestsellers, and beamed at a delirious pack of fans yet to emerge. My flaming artist heart pumped with glee.

One day, sporting my new portrayal, I pranced downtown into the hub of the professional world to clear up a discrepancy at the bank. Black coat. Black hat. Black boots. Silver earrings flashing like quick fish in cold streams. Hair free of buns, barrettes, and barricades. A far cry from the dehydrated pearls, pumps that felt like pizza ovens on warm days, pinching wristwatch, and Evan Picone suits of my previous incarnation. I was feeling like a visitor to my old world from a planet in outer space, out of the office orbit— planet Artist. I was relishing the contrast between my former life and my budding, brilliant, redemptive existence. Until . . .

Until I spied Clarence Whiting, a six-foot-tall senior partner from Smith & Hudson. I tried not to look at him in his accusing pinstripe, but he saw me. I stared at the velvet rope at my side, thinking that maybe I could just *will* him into a parallel universe, but feeling his gaze remain in my direction. God, what would his eyes behold? Immediately, I felt myself shrinking into my cape. The feathered hat on my head now felt like a baby kangaroo or a bowl of spoiling fruit. I wanted to rip that flag off my head, wish myself into a navy blue suit, or disappear into a knot in the wood paneling. Standing there for the entire world to see, I felt like a seven-year-old playing grownup; worse yet, a young grownup woman playing grownup. I should not have left the house dressed like this, and now my ridiculous confidence had brought me to this red-hot, staining moment where there was nowhere to run and nowhere to stand.

"Tama? Tama, how are you?" Clarence asked, catching up with me in the lobby. He smiled as he took in the entirety of my outfit. "How's life outside the war zone? Found another job yet? What are you doing with yourself?" He made casual conversation, social conversation, then glanced at his watch and furrowed his great silver brows. "You look great, just like Annie Hall," he called back as he sailed out of the lobby and onto his next million-dollar, international, power-broker type meeting where absolutely no one would be wearing a feathered hat.

> And the more I heralded the fresh and quirky self that I loved, the more I felt as naked as a stone.

Clarence meant the "Annie Hall" remark kindly—his brown eyes had smiled—but the words stung like a scraped shin and I could feel my face turning as pink as bubble gum melting in the sun. Instantly, I read into his remark a humorous indulgence, like a daddy tickled by his dizzy little girl. In my theatrical cape and hat straight from the toy box, I felt like that dismissible child. Of course, I played this three-minute scene over and over in my mind a thousand times as I wept on the cold steering wheel of my Honda. Yet Clarence hadn't called me foolish. *I did.* Only I borrowed his authoritative, real-world eyes through which to see the flamboyant and misguided woman who was throwing her life away in favor of playing dress-up.

We will face these kinds of "tests" in our transition. A living declaration of independence entails a process of reclaiming and respecting the identities we've always denied or discounted. We didn't stand behind those disconcerting and "embarrassing" selves before. In fact, we stuffed diplomas and bonuses in their mouths and buried them alive. Our allegiance comes no easier now.

I had always loved and feared my own eccentricity. I admired the unusual, yet cringed at the outcast. I wanted to stand out, but needed to fit in. During my transition, I came to realize that the more honestly I became myself, the less easily I could homogenize into all cultures and circles. I couldn't look and be like everyone else and still stay true to myself. The queen chameleon had to step down from her throne. And the more I heralded the fresh and quirky self that I loved, the more I felt as naked as a stone.

But the vulnerability passes and in its wake comes realness. At first, trying on new lives feels like playing "make believe." But as we act out our new roles, we will *make belief*. We become solid with experience and poised and affirmed. We act with clarity and it no longer feels like confession. We come down from extreme positions because we rise in self-possession.

I no longer wear a black cape or crystals to convince myself of my creativity. I do announce myself as an artist and I do look people straight in the eyes, even if they're wearing pinstripe suits and ties. In general, I no longer feel like I am broadcasting a strange and dangerous lifestyle. This unconventional life no longer feels superior or inferior. It mostly feels just right for me and transcendent and normal all at the same time.

Go ahead and experiment and play. Become a character in your story. Let new identities roar from the rooftops. Go way too far. Lean into living a new way.

We all go through the teenage years. We all outgrow them, too. Stomp, holler, and bellow your desire. You'll catch your balance when you catch on fire.

Let A Tiger Guard The Temple Of Your Time

*"I am coming to see that time free is not indulgence, but a kind
of vigilance. Knowing myself and knowing my dreams comes
from having time. Without self-connection,
I won't have true direction."*
A journal entry

~

*"The most important thing is to hold on, hold out,
for your creative life, for your solitude, for your time
to be and do, for your very life."*
Clarissa Pinkola Estés

Your commitment to time-out in a keep-hopping, no-stopping, lazy-phobic society will challenge you. Few of us "follow our bliss" without squirming and waiting for the productivity police to bust us in mid-ease, and haul us away to irresponsibility prison where we will eat gruel and master the rules of austerity. Not working the insane hours, and then on top of that spending good money on fringe-type workshops, books, and tapes, can sound like madness, especially when sadness has felt familiar and safe. But nothing is more important during this time than taking time to know yourself once again, giving yourself the space for self-revelation to take place.

During my time off, guilt played a tuba in the background of all my activities. When others rushed off to hectic jobs, I would amble off to the park to sit in the autumn sun with my new co-workers and glistening cohorts, the geese and mallards by the lake. I'd watch children holding their mothers' hands and old men in wool coats and caps tossing peanuts to squirrels and pigeons. I relished the time, but felt embarrassed about its value, *my* value.

Of course, I never asked these kinds of questions when I stared into space or tore little shreds of yellow legal paper at my desk on the thirtieth floor. As a workaholic attorney, my days would blur into one another like a swath of melted time. I'd work through lunch and drink lattes without tasting the sweetness or the warmth. I'd ride the bus home at night and stare out into the blackness and not see a single thing. And every week I'd collect this check that assured me that, though I reeled through my life in an efficient stupor, I need never wonder about my significance to society. But those days lacked value to me. They lacked a connection to my essence, my core self, the part of me that walked in purple robes out in the sage grasses of poetry and possibility.

In contrast, strolling past elm trees and evergreens on a Tuesday morning, I felt a sense of significance. Sitting on a weathered bench, journaling, asking myself the most important questions of my lifetime felt clean and honorable. The sun beamed and I warmed with appreciation for taking this time out to find out who I was and where my real life called me to go.

A period of self-discovery is a lot like falling in love. No one pays you for your commitment to wandering in the old rose garden of your own enchantment and birthright. Yet you won't *do* anything, at least not in this lifetime, that provides more value.

Guilt wastes precious time. Guilt's twin, false "productivity," eats hours, too. I hate to break this to you, but you did not quit your career to organize your closets, help your husband with his business, stay on the phone with co-dependent friends, pick up the neighbor's kid from school, hit the sales at department stores, or re-tile your bathroom. You do not have time for coffee klatches of gossip

> Of course, you still have responsibilities, but be responsible with them. You'll know when you've cleaned a closet as a crutch or run an errand to run away from yourself.

and lament. You do not have "free time," but time you pay for excavating dreams and navigating means.

Believe me, distraction and the itsy-bitsiest hope of validation will seem almost irresistible to you as you pull back from your old responsibilities and externally driven life. When the mythical hero Odysseus sailed past the seductive and illusionary Sirens that would attempt to lure him into the rocks, he asked his men to tie him down.

I am asking you to do the same thing. Tie yourself down to being as untied to ordinary life as possible. Sail the unfamiliar seas of unabashed time. Ignore the voices that will shame you into cleaning out the garage instead of ambling around an art gallery basking in colors and shapes and undiluted encounters of the soul. Sure, you can answer the question, "So what did you do today?" with something ordinarily laudable that makes everyone feel safe and comfortable. But while this is a journey of elbowroom and euphoric puttering, it is not one of comfort. We are bucking the tide of a workaholic society and listening to the renegade rivers of our creative spirits instead.

Of course, you still have responsibilities, but be responsible with them. You'll know when you've cleaned a closet as a crutch or run an errand to run away from yourself. And you'll do this and it's no big deal. Just bring yourself back when you can. As in the practice of Zen meditation, come back to your breath, your posture, and the purpose of this time.

This is womb time, a time of safety and extra-rich nurturance, meant to feed a precious new life that grows strong and wondrous only when given what it needs to grow strong and wondrous.

This is dream-beckoning time, smoothing out the nets and holding tight the line. This is not idle time, but unbridled time—time to invite visions and missions through the prayer of your willingness and the stance of your permission.

To the untrained eye, it may look like empty space. But as you begin to reclaim your strength, you will know that this was the time in which everything good and true took place.

⌒

You May Have To Leave Home To Come Home

The Fallen Children

We are the fallen children.
We dared to look for light.
We did not have the right.
Do not have right lives.
We are the fallen ones our loved ones
groan to tell of now.
And when they ache and spill, stoop shouldered
neighbors sag their heads.

We are the fallen,
falling outside in,
recalling what we are not,
recalling what we are not.

We touched the light, but we forgot,
recalling what we are not,
recalling what we are not.

Tama J. Kieves

*S*ometimes in transition, you can feel crazy, damaged, and isolated. But if you really want to feel crazy, damaged, and isolated, turn to family members or friends who may not understand your journey and ask them for support. It's a natural instinct to want certain people to be there for you. But they may not know the ways of going nova. My mother once called me a masochist because I chose to go to therapy and talk about things that made me cry. From her perspective, that made sense. But it wasn't what the searching part of me needed to hear. I was looking for something more along the lines of a "there, there, dear."

If you want to save time, I suggest you do not knock on doors that do not open to you. You only come away with raw knuckles and a scraped heart. For a while, I insisted on believing my parents would "see the light" and cheer me on in my new and dazzling choices. Calling Brooklyn every other weekend, I reasoned, "Well, if I relate my story a little better, then they'll get it." "If I use other words, then they'll get it." But always the sad, sad gut-clenching silence. Then one day revelation stung me. "No, Tam, it's you who won't get it. They hear you fine. You're just not hearing what you want from them."

Loved ones may lack the therapeutic instinct to give you the space, encouragement, and support you need. Your choices might frighten or threaten them. You are shooting for the moon and alignment in the cosmos when all they ever wanted to do was put food on the table and warm blankets on their beds. Passion wasn't one of their job requirements. I remember once my mother asking me in desperation, "What do you want me to say? Do you want me to say I'm thrilled when I'm not or that I understand when I don't?" Good point. She shouldn't have had to value my values while I was casually discarding hers.

Likewise, many old friends can't walk with us into our luminous new worlds. They may fear us walking beyond *our* fears and can even see this as an indictment of themselves. Or sometimes their extra-heavy burdened concern for us, their deep-set eyes, and the way they play with their pinky rings, can feed our suspicions instead of our sense of mission. Clarissa Pinkola Estés, champion of adventurers, put it this way, "When seeking guidance, don't ever listen to the tiny hearted."

We do need support during these unfamiliar times. But not just any support. Because well-meaning people will say well-meaning things that will make us feel foreign and tilted for wanting to walk this world another way. We need our own to walk us home. These people have chosen to follow the brightness in their own lives. They recognize the light in us because they do not look from fright.

Believe me, you will know your own. I remember attending a lecture with Jean Houston, an international speaker who

> Well-meaning people will say well-meaning things that will make us feel foreign and tilted for wanting to walk this world another way.

combines science, philosophy, and spirituality to rouse audiences with her imperative presence. At the time, I didn't know anything about Houston and I hesitated to attend the presentation. I had had it in mind to stretch out on my beige couch and feel sorry for myself rather than squeeze between a hundred other people on wooden chairs at a local church so I could expose myself to something new. But I showed up because I had a free ticket, a friend who nudged me to go with him, and a hunger for alternative perspectives.

This woman who I'd never heard of before reminded me of myself, my best self, the self I sought, the self I would become by stepping beyond the world I'd come from. I felt this ancient knowing inside being warmed and soothed and cradled into magnitude. I sat at the edge of my seat, alive to every word, my heart panting within my chest. Breathe. Breathe. Breathe. I had forgotten to breathe. I was coming alive into a larger life. This woman stormed across the stage, announcing the soul's roll call for me. Inside, a sleeping self jolted to attention.

What did she talk about? She talked about the "passion for the possible," about doing your dreams, about now, now, now, do it, do it, do it. It was a pure dose of the support I needed. I remember leaving that auditorium resolving to leave behind the waterlogged relationships in my life, the naysayers, the "someday" sayers, and the ones who wanted to talk about other things as though I had other things to talk about. I wanted to know the Jean Houstons, Marianne Williamsons, and other motivational speakers before they became the published authors and visionary leaders on stage. I wanted live wires in my life instead of those who pulled the plug on my desires. I looked around at the audience and felt more of a connection to these "strangers" than to many of the friends I'd been trying to educate into supporting me. There are other people like me ready to become, I thought. No longer will I ask the darkened ones how to leave the dark. I will find my own to walk me home.

Some of "my own" came from passages in books. I discovered comrades and brethren in authors I'd never met. These form-less friends did not drench me with the details of a situation they would never do anything about. They wrote from the road. They shared their pains and gains the moment we met, and I felt the ease that enters when isolation leaves. At times when everyday small talk surrounded me, a wailing emptiness to my ears, I clung to the words in books, the milestones, landmarks, and kinship of fellow travelers.

Later, I found new inspirations in classes and support groups. I even started my own support groups. Allies appeared and told the same soul stories of stepping out of bounds and of finding new ground. Over and over, it would amaze me that I would win support for my new life *in* my new life. But that's how it happened. And finding a place where I belonged, I grew strong— strong enough to go home and hold my own.

I don't believe we are meant to boycott our families and old friends in the name of following our dreams. But I do believe that transitional times charge us with unique needs.

Transition is a time of close concentration like walking a tight rope. Yes, maybe it's even a little obsessive. But we don't have the luxury of life on the periphery. Our lives depend upon this walk and we're a little sensitive about each step.

We will calm down. We will come down.

But first we need what we need when we dare to walk this higher ground.

I Pledge Allegiance
to Myself

Chapter Six

*H*old it. Stop right there. You with those casually cruel perceptions of yourself. If you want a ticket to the promised land, you'll have to leave that ranting creativity killer at the gate. You know, that advisor of treason that you call "reason." Did you think you could do what you love in the same bruising way you did what you hated? Sure you did.

But you can't. Self-criticism keeps you small and self-absorbed. You might whip yourself into remorse, but never into the kind of crescendo that lifts density into genius. Just try an attitude of severity and watch creativity flee your room, your house, and your aura for days on end. That's right. Your relationship with yourself determines your flow and the quality of love that shines in your work. So, if you want razzle-dazzle, quit those frazzled attempts to beat yourself into magnificence. Creativity thrives on kindness and self-care.

And when the night is really dark, give yourself a lot of room.

Only trust calls down the moon.

Only The Tender Can Breed The Fierce

"Turn your face to the sun and the shadows fall behind you."
A Maori proverb

~

*"Come, come whoever you are, wanderer, worshipper, lover of leaving,
it doesn't matter. Ours is not a caravan of despair.
Come, even if you have broken your vow a thousand times.
Come, come yet again, come."*
Rumi

I watched the waves crash against the shore. "Crash against me," I thought. "I'm pathetic and defeated." I'd had a pretty low self-esteem day on vacation in Northern California. My friend and I had gone hiking in the Redwood Forest and my latest insecurities had run away with my will and the useful part of my mind. I had this wild fear of getting lost deep in the woods with no way out, an implausible fantasy that only some kind of possessed person would heed. I heeded. Despite trail markers and other assurances of safety, I beat my way back to the rental car in the parking lot. There I burned in the inner fires of shame. I'd missed much of the Redwood Forest because my crazy fear had overcome my good judgment and my eagerness to see new beauty. It was just like my writing career. I turned back from what I really wanted over and over again.

Miles and hours later, I was sitting, glaring, at dark, craggy rocks with a vehement ocean smashing against them. I perched high on a barnacle-covered boulder, wiggling my toes, beholding the sun set, observing some rays light up ripples in a calmer region of the gray-blue water. My eyes rested on the gentleness, the slow laps, the easy waves, and the pink light casting silver rose petals across a liquid, lapping canvas. I quieted inside, mesmerized, not surprised when the ocean spoke in a voice without sound. "Be kind," said the presence, "be very kind." My eyes blinked with tears as the rest of the sentence rolled in like a majestic scroll unfolding. "Be kind to you."

"Be kind to you." The ocean spoke with a sweep of magnitude and a suppleness that could polish rocks and shells and broken hearts and driftwood. "Be even kinder to yourself when you feel fear. Love, not anger, inspires right action. It takes tenderness to breed the fierce."

Boy, tenderness wasn't exactly what I'd had in mind. I loathed what I perceived as weakness. All my life, I'd thrown spitballs at my fragile self and stuck chewed-up gum on the seat of her chair. Left to my own "enlightened" devices, I was about as willing to embrace my weak spots as I was to eat a piece of tenderloin turning green.

But the ocean's guidance reminded me how I'd already seen successes born of care and strong compassion. I thought of a friend who rescues abandoned kittens. Feral, dirty, and mistrusting of the world, these animals huddle in alleys, near dumpsters, or in the dark and dry margins of people's back porches. Only patience and perseverance persuades these suspicious creatures to forsake their chosen corners. My friend coaxes them with bowls of milk, quiet movements, and silky tones. Sometimes she leaves food for them and doesn't even attempt an approach for days. Eventually, a sly and shrinking one will face danger because it senses the promise and safety of an ally. My friend would not think to yell at a shivering animal or taunt it because it hesitated. Of course, neither would I. But I would think nothing of yelling at the unsure part of myself and sending it darting back into unavailability.

For years, I'd known about my inner child, its warps and wounds and latent magic. I'd read the self-help and psychology books that told me to get in touch with this inner child, keeper of the sparkles. But no one had ever told me how to act like an encouraging inner parent. I didn't know how to supervise myself without a meat cleaver

Be even kinder to yourself when you feel fear. Love, not anger, inspires right action.

in one hand, a cutting board in the other, and every moment of my life in between. I actually thought that all that slicing and dicing would foster wholeness. I never noticed how much my own criticism encouraged me to feel small and helpless, and how much the bully in my brain laid into me for exactly that, feeling small and helpless.

But in this instant of benediction, the ocean swelled with an allowance and a generosity that could accept my imperfections as no big deal. The great open water offered its love to me even if I'd chosen to back out of an adventure that ten thousand other people would not have turned away from. The ocean accepted me even if back home I'd had this approach/avoidance dance going on with my writing—even if some days I barely wrote, or I wrote poorly, or I crawled into a ball and stared at the wall.

The ocean judged no part of me as reproachable or undeserving of welcome or kindness. My sense of shame began to lift and scatter on the breeze like sea foam or dried debris. The knots within me loosened, my shoulders softened, chalices clinked within, and I returned to sanity and self-respect. I glimpsed on that rock, in one quiet moment, the power and promise of an unconditional champion and friend.

Suddenly, I wanted to give to myself in a new way; forgive myself for my frailties, my lapses in brightness, my cold-engine mornings. Forgiveness would help me get on with action instead of drowning in my own backlash and reaction. The bully that had always called me names and elbowed and shoved me forward never made me feel like I *could* move on ahead. But in a moment of acceptance, a simple "hey, it's all right," it *was* all right. It was no big deal. I could begin again. And I could approach a bowl of milk, a writing assignment, or a wooded trail in my own skittish and adorable timing.

"Be kind to you," the ocean said once more. I knew I had encountered an infinite elder or wise one, the reflection of a nurturing voice within me, who would teach me the mystical ways of unconditional love even when I returned home to Colorado. I had begun to glimpse what it felt like to have someone on my side inside, someone who believed in my strength and invincibility and even my majesty and destiny when I stumbled and fell and believed in less. "Thank you," I said out loud.

I could feel dusk's chill like the breath of a cave moving in upon my arms and legs. The daystar set with a final blaze of pink and rust. But as I scrambled down from my rock, I was sure the sun had just begun to rise.

Master Approving Instead Of Improving

"Creation is a sentient and instinctual flow that determines where to go and what to change or omit."
Shaun McNiff

～

"A singed bird does not sing."
A journal entry

*O*ur culture doesn't exactly steer us in the direction of trusting ourselves. We are taught from an early age to guard against, rather than revel in, our natural instincts. We are told we might get ahead of ourselves or behind ourselves—or worst of possible fates—be blind to ourselves. But, of course, I'm about to suggest the blasphemous. I'm about to tell you that you don't need improvement as much as you require attunement. And attunement comes from trusting more than self-adjusting.

I remember attending this writing critique group because some friends told me I'd better get feedback on my efforts lest I create something distorted by following my own lights. So I sat on a worn plaid couch in the cold basement of a local church on Wednesday nights. The critique group poured over each other's work, and then debated about where the writing in question needed wings or commas. I ate too many unsweetened oatmeal cookies and even nibbled on my Styrofoam teacup as I witnessed a jury trial over the placement of a semicolon.

Many of these budding writers offered interesting sugges-tions. They were nice people. They had nice children and spouses, and they even gave to charities and recycled their newspapers and aluminum cans in purple plastic bins on Thursdays. But that didn't matter to me. What mattered was that, once all those opinions started flying, I felt less inspired to write and more inspired to check all the details of my insurance polices to make sure I was really covered from hazards like tornadoes and floods and locusts and plagues. Maybe it was all the talk of mistakes and fine inten-tions gone awry. I don't know. What I do know is this: Like vul-tures, we'd peck at the carcass of a piece until we lost all sight of its feathers and flight. I'd leave the meetings feeling robbed of my time and like I'd gotten tangled in string and pulled down the kite.

Because as I drove up my driveway in the mountains and looked into the voluptuous night sky with its bone white moon, I always thought I could have written a poem instead of shuffling my feet and eating Styrofoam. I could have parted the seas and picked up seashells and words and let the sky pour warm, silky rain on my head as I slipped into sentences and meaning and touched my own heart. I ached to enter the kingdom of creativity and stroll round the gardens until I heard my own royal voice. Fi-nally, I realized I would never find my own voice by picking apart writing to find the flaws and reveal the laws. Correction just didn't bring me to *connection*, and connection is where my writing got big and barefooted and bolted toward the golden country.

It took me a long time to accept my creative process. My process was learning to *approve* of myself first before I tried to *improve* myself. I had to tell myself over and over, "You're doing everything right sweetheart. Just give me more, more, more, more of you. Stop looking over your shoulder and look only to your heart." I needed ongoing permission to stumble as well as to sprout improbable wings. So I had to create this voice inside myself, this

> Self-advocacy will take you farther down the road than any raspy-voiced meager critic or uptight, corseted perfectionist with pursed lips and hands on hips.

huge and forgiving net like a new, proud mother coaxing her diapered project to careen across the carpet for the first time.

I suggest you give yourself unheard-of latitude. Self-advocacy will take you farther down the road than any raspy-voiced meager critic or uptight, corseted perfectionist with pursed lips and hands on hips. Or maybe you like to learn by having ice water thrown in your face. All I know is I'm a lot more apt to keep working when I think my work has a shot of going somewhere. And as long as I keep working, I *create* that shot of it going somewhere. It's one of those twinkling laws of a mysterious and mirthful universe.

Think about children. If an eager child presents you with her masterpiece, her blotchy purple drawing, you could say, "What a mess. You need to improve your composition and lines." Or you might say instead, "What a free picture! Such lush color!" Both reactions honor the truth. Which comment will make the child more likely race back to her crayons, joyfully begin another picture, and improve from her practice? I'd say the one who feels like she has something to give and has already made a start; she has mastered freedom and strong color. The other child, cut down instantaneously, may put his art supplies and his spontaneity away, and later become an adult that locks his heart in a safe deposit box and then forgets the combination.

Support will not leave us naïve or inflated, or with blotchy drawings all our lives. We will not work in the dark without a hawkeyed teacher, but in the light. Experience teaches. I have found that the act of writing taught me how to write. The page became my guru and my tour guide. As with any practice, I grew fluid as I grew earnest. Dedication came to me because I felt like I was making progress. Then the creative force within me stretched for artistic purity, and found joy in correction, enlightenment, and refinement. The puma seeks maximum grace. Real creativity takes us beyond ego. But first we have to get beyond fear. We have to want to go back and pick up our crayons.

So here's my take on things. Develop and ply what you have instead of what you don't have. Feed your strengths. Pet the tigers. Don't worry about the amoebas. Because they will develop in their own time.

Meanwhile, light small votive candles on the altars of your gifts. The worship of your strength will make you strong. Please do not cut yourself to shreds in the name of improvement. First seek movement. Then seek movement. Again, seek movement.

Grow wild and wooly before you prune.

Have faith in the living wisdom of your talent, and it will light your way as surely as the moon.

Quixotic Means To Exotic Work

"Let the way that you work love you. Let the way conform to your own holy nature instead of squeezing yourself into tight places or giving yourself so much space you drift away."
A journal entry

⌒

"Discipline means being a disciple to yourself."
A journal entry

*N*ow, no longer do we have to squeeze our aliveness into somebody else's cubicle or work style or hours. But how do you begin to work and how do you touch the fire? Do you work in an evening gown or your underwear, in an office, a warehouse, or a beanbag chair? I think we all want a clinical formula for productivity. But on this path, real effectiveness comes from authenticity. Ditch any standard or expectation that doesn't come from your heart. Just get to know yourself exquisitely well and let your instincts take you to your art.

Sometimes you will need a sense of permission as big as Texas. And sometimes you'll have to tighten the reins to keep yourself from prancing away from the encounter you really want. And maybe you will need to adjust your style midstream again and again. It doesn't matter what you do. It matters that you choose whatever way you work because it nourishes you and feels true.

When I first began writing, I industriously studied books on how to write. Perky little student with hands-folded-on-her-desk that I am, I sampled some of the programs of famous writers. Hemingway rose at 6:00 A.M. to pen his vigorous classics. I admired Hemingway's crisp style, so I braved his crisp schedule. It didn't exactly make me want to fight bulls, although I did notice a marked increase in my desire to perpetrate violence.

And that's about as creative as I got. I can't figure out how to concoct instant coffee before 10:00 A.M., much less brew up eloquent sentences or stories. My macho mornings didn't last long. Neither did my afternoon and evening schedules. No routine endured. After "billing time" as an attorney, something in me refused to measure my life by the little black arrows of some invention that had no idea how many hours I really needed to live a particular day. Instead, I wrote when I felt like it, in spurts and phases—bursts of enthusiasm, then lulls. I slunk about in randomness, nagging myself to commit to more structure. How could I call myself a devoted writer if I had no consistent work routine? More importantly, how could I trust myself to complete work?

Then I tried what I dubbed the "temperamental artist method." I decided on the number of pages or a specific product I desired by the end of the week. I could write in the afternoon one day and at night the next. I could take days off and then work another day straight past evening and into those strange hours when birds start singing the darkness into light. I could do whatever I wanted so long as I met my goal or I consciously made a new and non-cop-out agreement with myself. Freedom agreed with me and my artist handed in her "assignments" on time.

Eventually, I abandoned even this structure. I just knew what felt like dedication and what didn't. I think it's like those people who cook. You ask them how they did something or what recipe they used and they tell you, "Oh, a little of this, a little of that, you know." Of course, since I don't cook, I look at them blankly as though they are deliberately withholding concrete information from me. But it's one of those art things. You slip into a groove or a zone and you know your own way home, even when you don't remember the address.

Now I do recommend a schedule for anyone who never seems to "find" time to develop the thing they say they want to do most with their lives. Let's face it, it's hard to find time. It's not like you're walking on the beach looking for abalone shells and you accidentally find an hour, or you're digging through old papers to find a phone number and you never find it, but you do come across a week. "Finding" is a very passive activity and not necessarily the way you want to treat something that has been so dire that you had to leave a good career and make your family worry about you and bug clergy members to pray for your professional salvation. It's not like you would take your child to the emergency room if you found the time, or pay your electric bill if you happened to find a month under the car seat. When hours and weeks run into one another, it may be time to give up the watercolor technique of life and switch to something more definite like acrylics.

"A schedule defends from chaos and whim," says Pulitzer Prize–winning author Annie Dillard. "It is a net for catching days." It can also represent a date with yourself, or with destiny or with those crackpot goddesses who lit this candle in your heart and said you could rouse a fire that would glint its way through dimness. Maybe structure or schedule is just the form of anchoring self-care you secretly crave. Personally, I can't think of a more merciful thing to do for yourself than to affirm your creative desires with constancy and dignity.

> It doesn't matter what you do. It matters that you choose whatever way you work because it nourishes you and feels true.

My mountain neighbor and friend, Lucy, declares the first four hours of her day a ritual of rigor and of comfort. She walks her black Labs through the awakening woods and sets her blood and brain singing, while people like me snore happily through the virtue hours of dew-strewn daybreak. Returning home, Lucy brews her coffee and sifts through a book of inspirational sayings and rejuvenating meditations. Then she sits down before her computer, plugs in her answering machine, and enters a dot-size town in West

Virginia, the locale of her book. Resistance greets her, as always. But she has habit as her searchlight and she makes her way through the fog just fine. Lucy doesn't look at her writing time as a chore or obligation. She sees it as a velvet box of chocolate-covered cherries and cremes, a luxury just for herself.

So there you have it. Two different extremes that accomplish the same thing, except that, to some, Lucy will appear more steadfast than I do. I'm sure there're another ten thousand options in between. In fact, I know I've straddled quite a few of them. But you get the idea.

Now it's up to you to experiment and invent. But mostly listen. Listen to what love would have you do. Fear and guilt do not belong in this equation. They have nothing to do with stirring up pots of inspiration.

Forget your grim images of work and responsibility. Pick an approach that, moment by moment, brings you comfort and sets you free.

All Movement Comes Of Trust

"I've never transcended what I haven't embraced."
Jon Marc Hammer

❧

"It's so hard to give up all trying. It goes against every grain of our Puri-
tan work ethic 'force-yourself-into-submission-even-if-it-kills-you'
model. It's hard to wait for the bus. It's hard to believe that another
moment will come that is different from this one.
It's so hard to be easy."
A journal entry

I had had a bad afternoon. No creative spice or juice. No faith. No energy. I'd waited tables the night before until closing. The next day, *my* day, I just couldn't make myself write. Since I'd even slept in, I didn't think I had a "right" to be tired or uninvolved. I felt like one of those gagged women tied up on the tracks eye-balling a steaming black locomotive barreling toward her. Like that train, my time was going to run out and run right over me because I couldn't untie myself and fly on paper.

"I give up. I just can't seem to get it together," I told my laid-back friend Kir over the phone. A desperation call. One of those "give me sympathy because I want to vent like a kettle" calls. He listened. Quiet. Inviting my story, the blow-by-blow details of nothing accomplished. "I walk around here. I walk to the fridge. Open the door, close it, then I come back with a vengeance and eat all the banana bread and feel worse. I just can't seem to write or think or function. I give up." Tears of failure and frustration thickened my voice.

"You say 'I give up,'" enlightenment boy said at just the appropriate time. "But you go on fighting yourself, demanding a certain outcome. Why not accept feeling tired?" The question hung there like a hatchet. "What?" I said. "Waste my writing time? Wallow in the mud? Just give up on my dreams, no questions asked?" Kir waited for my rebel to quiet down and listen.

"No. If you feel tired, respect your experience and stop judging yourself. Why not honor feeling tired? Rent a pile of videos. Fix some buttered popcorn. Crash on the couch. Care for the worn-out part of yourself and that worn-out feeling will move through. Everything that is loved is freed."

Oh. The old "embrace the feeling totally" and you move through it like Ram Dass or some orange-robed monk whose most exalted ambition in life is to follow his breath into nirvana. Personally, I'd always thought that therapists spread these kinds of theories around at trade conventions while shopping for softer couches. Well, I had to admit that my Trooper Jane "I will overcome myself" mentality hadn't produced much poetry lately and did have me groveling in the desert for alternatives.

Okay, I resolved. I'll give my love even to this moment. It sounded like such a Zen thing to do. But I could feel a largeness behind the curtain of my cynicism. It felt like someone had just slipped me a tall glass of lemonade just when I was going to pass out from heat stroke. Of course, I had denied myself the water all along because I was stubborn enough to do that, and misguided enough, too. Finally, I could abandon the bushy-tailed scenarios in my head in which an alternative me was writing for *The Atlantic Monthly* while doing laundry, dishes, and calisthenics, and probably dating someone stupendous, too, with connections in the publishing world and film industry, not to mention his family's vineyards and villa in Tuscany.

> When all my defeated expectations trudged out of the day taking their jackhammers and chainsaws with them, my heart's desire could just quietly bloom.

So I put the would-be great American Pulitzer Prize–winning short story aside and nuked up a mountain of popcorn in my favorite purple plastic bowl. I sunk into the forbidden land of late afternoon and early evening television. It felt weird not to have a fever or runny nose as a passport, but I managed to give myself this reprieve without the obligatory harassment.

Hours later, because I hadn't torn myself apart with judgment, I found myself rested, the best I'd felt all week. And then the amazing happened. I actually felt like writing. Let me say that again. I actually felt like writing. It was just there all by itself. I didn't have to light a fire under my computer, do a rain dance, don my hair shirt, invoke novenas, or anything. The desire just welled up within me like a perfect red poppy. I think it came because it finally had the room. When all my defeated expectations trudged out of the day taking their jackhammers and chainsaws with them, my heart's desire could just quietly bloom.

I learned a lot about treating myself with trust and respect that rundown Thursday. Until then, I'd always handled myself with righteous suspicion, guarding against this inner lowlife in its stained trench coat, just waiting to slip me a bad bus token and screw up my chances for a full and useful life. But all that guarding against myself didn't exactly inspire the big-spirited productivity extravaganza I'd had in mind. Low opinions of myself generated low energy and low energy wore house slippers all day, and never put her toes in the chilling waters of vibrant creative connection.

Your integrity knows when it's time to brave resistance and when it's time to brave a movie and a bowl of popcorn instead. Self-respect inspires self-honesty. Let go of your wariness. And try on a bias of trustworthiness.

You will gravitate toward your dream. You will find the secret stream. You come because you want to, you have to, you burn inside when you feel denied.

I know it seems like sacrilege to stop trying. But I know no other way to begin to *fly*.

All movement comes of trust. Everything else is just a useless brawl and fuss.

When You Nurture Yourself, You Nurture Your Dreams

"Everybody assumes that when you don't work nine to five, you have a lot of time for relaxation. But not working and resting are two different things. I feel the twin tensions of uncertainty and birth pressing upon me incessantly. Sometimes I think a board meeting or a trial would be more relaxing."
A journal entry

⌒

"Every perceived threat implores me to connect with the awesome and indestructible essence within me."
A journal entry

*W*ithin one week, three rejection letters had stung me and I stumbled around the house in sweatpants, wondering if and when my life would ever come together. I put the envelopes away and dried my tears, but I could not sit down and write. I was trapped again in the cobwebs of anxiety, those sticky beliefs that retire in certain angles of light, only to glare in others: "Maybe I lack that special something to break into a creative career." "Maybe I'll never make any money." "Maybe I should just give up." Winter's bleary skies didn't help.

So, for my birthday, I decided to use an unexpected check from my parents to help buy myself an unusual gift. I decided to rent a cabin near Rocky Mountain National Park for three days. Three days of solitude, mountain air, and space away from city life, my life, the same four walls with the same blank stares and mute accusations.

The wind howled and snow flurries whirled about as I pulled into the Estes Park center's grounds. After stopping at the main lodge to register, I stepped into my cabin, my rustic retreat from the storm. The thick walls and low ceiling seasoned the air with cedar and the varnished beams exposed knots and grain like a petrified watercolor painting. From the window, I could see the blue snowcapped Rockies and three burly Ponderosa pines. The main room provided a small round table, three lean, wooden chairs, an upholstered printed rocker, and a fading blue couch. All the essentials awaited. Nothing extra.

Everything about the place suggested cleanliness as brisk as the air outside. I welcomed the sparseness and purity. It felt as though a lumberjack with a plaid shirt had just finished hammering in the nails and a little missus in a bonnet had scurried about to tidy up and tuck a tattered Bible into the nightstand drawer. No radio. No television. No clock. And no responsibilities. Just falling snow. Magnificent wind. And me.

I didn't end up walking around the grounds or into the national park as much as I planned. I could say the snow deterred me. But it seems as though I wanted to be deterred. I spent most of my time on that blue couch devouring self-help books about writing and creativity while my windowpane frosted. I remember thinking, "You're spending money to sit on a couch and read?" But reading seemed like the thing to do.

Gradually I sunk into the space, holed up in my womb of a cabin, in a blanket of quietness, protected by snow and thick beams of wood. I stopped fighting myself, pushing myself to walk or write or instantly settle down into my expectation of tranquility. I read and I cried and I stared at pine trees. It seemed like the thing to do.

That night I prepared a simple dinner of broiled chicken and brown rice. A warm and rich aroma of cooking and contentment suffused the cabin and suddenly I felt as though I had come home to myself. Somehow the act of cooking a wholesome meal for just me tugged at my heart. A mother's love puttered and clanged in the kitchen. And I was receiving the love. I stepped out onto the small porch and looked up at the dark night sky. The snow had stopped and a thousand faraway diamonds pierced the crisp blackness. I breathed in the air, so cold it stung my lungs, clear and sweet and spiced with smoke from the lodge's chimney. I absorbed the presence of quiet, a stillness as dominating as a lion, and in that moment my troubles drifted off into eternity, a trillion miles away. I was right here in heaven under a star-filled sky with a good meal cooking in my kitchen and a novel waiting by a warm and firm bed. No rejection letter in the world could threaten the goodness of this moment in time. I felt unharmed and once again invincible.

That trip broke my spell of doubts and heaviness and the larger pattern I'd had in my life of only being nice to myself when I had succeeded at something. This time I had given myself a gift, not a reward or a bribe. I didn't have it all together. I hadn't finished a clever short story or sold an article to *The New Yorker* or even a local Colorado publication. I hadn't done anything to "deserve" to go away. But I gave myself a gift of peace in the middle of an arduous journey, a pause to catch my breath and my balance during an uphill climb.

At the end of my three days, I left the cabin feeling spiritually nourished and restored to wholeness. I found myself eager to start over, send out more manuscripts, and write new ones. Far away from rejection letters and file folders of incomplete stories, I came to *believe* again; I came to want my dream again. Because the more I relaxed, the more I returned to the creative instinct within me, as natural and as enduring as the pine trees by my window. Far away from my fears and frustrations, I could feel the knowing of my heart. My truth would triumph over the temporary reproaches of reality. Like those

> This time I had given myself a gift, not a reward or a bribe.

trees, my branches might tilt in the wind, but I would not tumble down or break apart.

The gift I gave myself had worked its magic. I had acted with spontaneous love and I had experienced love's startling power. Despite the same exact facts waiting for me in Denver, I believed again in my calling, my path, and the wholeness within myself. More importantly, I knew then that if I dug down deeply, sighed loudly, and rested when weary, self-love could see me through any and every aspect of this journey.

Every Rosebud Starts
in the Mud

Chapter Seven

*O*f course you will agitate yourself with the age-old question, "What if I'm no good?" What if I'm just a toad on paper or on canvas or in the marketplace? And I have absolutely no doubt that you will be a toad, a bomb, and a disappointment to yourself. Because genius does not often arrive as genius, but as imperfection tolerated and transformed by love, focus, and devotion.

Sure, we all want to wake up as royalty and never mop a floor as long as we live. You know, glory without labor. But we all begin as peasants—blunted and coarse and groping for splendor.

But grope on. The splendor comes.

Because we who are awkward, hapless, small, and slow are also gifted, transcendent, radiant, and glittering.

We are crowned when we are called.

And we **will** fly. But first we crawl.

You Don't Have To Be Someone Special To Be Someone Special

"That was it; I was nobody. And since I was nobody, there was nobody to acknowledge—no one to name, much less honor such a thing as—a gift."
Nancy Aronie

⌒

"We come to recognize that God is unlimited in supply and that everyone has equal access."
Julia Cameron

So many of us think success happens to other people, different people, gleaming people, people of a favored species or gene pool. But everyone starts off human. Two feet. Two hands. One gorgeous heart of infinite power and promise.

For instance, I thought that becoming a published writer was about as probable as my ascending Mount Everest. It's one of those things that's theoretically possible, just like becoming president or first lady or achieving balance in this lifetime. But it never happens to you or anyone you know in your women's howl-at-the-moon support group.

To become a published writer, I just knew I had to have some kind of college roommate/lover in the mailroom of Harper-

Collins, or an uncle who had helped a senior editor get his son out of a cult or out of jail. Failing that, I had to reside in New York City and attend parties *du jour* in warehouses and lofts, eat sushi, wear black on black on black, and quote beat poets. My mind swam with images of grainy-faced reporters sucking scotch and cigars, and deranged, uncanny poets with stringy hair and dilated pupils.

Each week, I pored over magazines in the local library memorizing bylines of people I didn't know. I read articles I wished I could have written, and then I read the paramount paragraph in italics at the end of each article that told about the staff writer or freelancer. Oh, those devastating printed names. The lucky ones. Established. Complete. Swinging on stars and validated, paid for their words, enjoying the luxury of artistic legitimacy on every day of every week. To me, published writers had walked in gardens I would never know and sipped jasmine tea with mint and credibility.

After worshipping enough bylines, I'd usually lay the magazine down or put a book back on the shelf, my heart heavy with unlived dreams, sorrow, and longing. I felt like the peasant girl who aches to go to the ball and maybe meet the prince, but she doesn't have a gown, an invitation, a fairy tale, or a prayer. Why would some New York City publisher want to deal with me? Right now the real writers were courting advances and assignments from editor pals over Thai food in "The Village," while I stood in Denver, a million miles away and way too close to Kansas, clutching my passionately written but doomed-to-peasant-life articles, short stories, and poems. I was an unknown commodity and I didn't have the right pickaxe or panache to break into the club.

Let's face it. I knew lawyers, real estate agents, word processors, and more lawyers. I didn't know people who considered their "hobbies" art or paths to bliss or (God forbid) secret missions embroidered with spiritual lessons and unseen allies. Published writers and acclaimed artists didn't live on my block. They had exotic conversations on some other planet. They skinny-dipped in moonlight and drank deep red wine. They collected pottery and fetishes and knew where to buy boots and hats. Mortals like me just didn't frolic in that great big poppy field of art as a profession.

But my presumptions were about to evolve the day I received a class catalog from a local adult education center. With butterflies in my stomach (and a few leftover caterpillars), I registered for "Creative Writing 101." The instructor had published fiction and non-fiction books and sold magazine articles to famous publications like *New Woman* and *Good Housekeeping*. She did not work at other jobs. She wrote for a living and had for quite some time. Seems like she had a home office on the tip of Mount Everest.

Entering the packed classroom, I looked for *the published author,* the queen of creative accomplishment, the one percent of the herd of humanity who actually turns dreams into wine and even bread on the table.

But I couldn't find anyone undeniable in the room. So I checked out my classmates and the clock on the pale gray wall.

Then I observed again some woman with beaded earrings and dyed hair at the head of the class. Her plump face acknowledged the audience. To my amazement, Hanna Richmond introduced herself as The One, the object of my awe and envy.

Meanwhile, Hanna Richmond spoke slowly, easily, escorting us into the enchanted kingdom of creative writing for the three-hour segment. During the break, she alluded to plumbing problems back at home. Good God! She had plumbing and plumbing problems! Then she yawned, revealing silver fillings.

As if all that weren't enough, I

This woman did not walk on water, but she did walk forward with heart.

happened to notice that a part of her hem hung longer than the rest of her denim, made-in-America, made-on-my-planet skirt. My mental circuits practically had a meteor shower within the tight little confines of my skull. I could hear books toppling off shelves in the library, like dominoes, like drum rolls, like the cosmos rearranging a few stars or planets into a stunning new order of the universe. The most extraordinary thing had just happened and had to be assimilated at once: *This writing guru was an ordinary woman.*

Suddenly, all the glamorous names in the library began to have noses, some with freckles, others long or broad. These "bylines" had arguments over pot roast and peas at the kitchen table. They had days when their pantyhose ran and evenings when they forgot their umbrellas. The rain fell on them, too, in big splotchy drops that trickled down those long, normal, air-breathing noses. And some of them even lived in places like Topeka and Toledo—and always had.

They had pocketed the moon anyway. These men and women had skyrocketed out of their ordinary existences of alarm clocks, office politics, cholesterol and dental bills into the stratosphere of lyrical lives. They had scrambled up the pearly staircase or wafted in on Turkish carpets. They had realized their luminous creative dreams—and mine. These ordinary humans. These mystical beings. These role models.

Blue birds began to chirp in my previously hardened heart as I watched this round woman scrawl recommended books on the board. I savored her drowsy voice. I adored her nose with two nostrils. I loved her hem best of all, the hem that straggled and tugged at my heart until my eyes welled with gratitude. I could identify with Hanna Richmond, and she had published articles and short stories and even paperback books and would write and publish more. This woman did not walk on water, but she had staved off the sea of compromise in which so many poetic souls had drowned. This woman did not walk on water, but she did walk forward with heart.

Something big and true became possible for me in that moment. Dreams didn't seem so beyond my reach. *I* could walk forward with heart. After all, I, too, had plumbing problems and silver fillings and unruly clothing. So maybe, just maybe, I could publish writing, touch the hem of the stars, and know an ordinary, extraordinary life of artistic realization.

You Must Be Small To Be Great

"We cannot see the mountain in the grain of sand, but we will see the grain of sand in the mountain."
A journal entry

~

"A tree that can fill the span of a man's arms grows from a downey tip; a terrace nine stories high arises from clods of earth; a journey of a thousand miles starts from beneath one's feet."
Lao-Tzu

My writing sounded like a kindergartner's compared to Barbara Kingsolver's or Pat Conroy's, so I figured why bother," Leslie sighed in a one-on-one coaching session. She stared with pained blue eyes at my patchwork blue pillow and at God-knows-what ugly scene in her mind, but a scene I know I'd seen. I'd been there before, in the place where ideals just crush you instead of inspire you. It's like you stop looking at the North Star as a guide and you start looking at it as a benchmark of your own light instead. Comparing your business potential or art to those who have already established themselves is cruel and pointless. Nobody starts out as a gold medallist. Nobody begins at the Grammys.

When I first started writing, I decided I would read every Steinbeck novel I could get my hands on because I loved that guy, loved his writing style and humanity-rich heart. So I read all the classics that I'd already read in high school and then I read some novels I'd never heard of, his earlier works that never made it into the limelight. And here's the amazing thing. His first novels were okay, but nothing to write term papers about, so to speak. I can't tell you how freeing I found this meek discovery. All of a sudden I found permission to write my short stories and essays even if I didn't write like Steinbeck. After all, even *John Steinbeck* didn't write like John Steinbeck in his new-kid-on-the-block years.

Perhaps you, too, suffer from this "instant master" syndrome, some persistent hallucination that the talented "greats" bounded from the cradle into unfathomable and crank-it-out proficiency. Well, last I heard, anyone who has ever realized a dream, has stayed awake at night, aching and praying, ripped up scientific theories and scores of music, paced, clutched at hope and lost it, opened another business, plummeted, sweated, dreamed, and envied other talented lights. Oh, and one other thing. They began. They hunkered down in their own less-than-perfect, museum-quality experience.

I remember visiting New York and catching the Broadway play *Gypsy* starring Tyne Daly. I sat transfixed in my velvet seat as she ripped through her audience like a gale of wind bows trees and flowers. She tore through our masks and barriers and defenses and moved us to tears, laughter, realizations, and what felt like altered states of consciousness. In response, we the audience clapped with glee. We rose from our seats and howled our adoration. We couldn't give enough or say thank you with enough thunder.

Later that night, still reeling with gratitude, swaying on a downtown D train, one of those blinding flashes of the obvious struck me. Tyne Daly *couldn't* have started there. She couldn't have gone to her very first acting class or audition and blasted away like that. But she had cared enough about her talent to get there. Something in me clicked. I wanted to reach that startling dimension with my own tender gifts. I wanted to be *that* good. I wanted to rise.

And finally I was willing to settle down and begin even with low self-esteem, cellulite, boredom, and this desperate, breathless need to make it to the top of the hill without anybody catching a glimpse of me in progress.

Greatness is born of our own inelegance befriended and assisted.

We must be small to be great. Greatness is born of our own inelegance befriended and assisted. If we can't allow ourselves to be bad, we will never allow ourselves to be good. It's that simple and shocking. Our egos hate this and shield their squinty little eyes from the light of this kind of truth. But there is a wise and genuine part of us that is willing to work with tolerance and produce ordinariness, inefficacy, and so-so results. This wise part knows the grace of things to come and that patience and compassion turn ordinariness into wine.

It's a sad and funny thing, but grandiosity actually chains us to inferiority. If we can't allow ourselves to be awkward and inept, then we will stay nothing but awkward and inept in one of those thin, dim hallways of creative purgatory. It's not a pretty sight.

So come to your work in your cotton robe. Sit before your talent in simple devotion. Let your actions be coarse and apparently fruitless. It takes a lot of "fruitless" actions to culminate in fruit. Practice with dignity. Grapple with humility. This is one of the greatest times in all of your creative career life. It takes such compassion and faith to work with blunted abilities while we covet big and flattering dreams.

Go ahead. It's time to start. Sculpt a vase that looks like a skinny chicken neck or teach a class that could be sold separately as a cure for insomnia. It doesn't matter. It's not the end of the world; it's the beginning.

If you wait for skill before you dare anything, you will only wait and ache. Yet proceed with simplicity and you will inch, then launch, toward proficiency. Don't ache to be great. Don't desire and wait. Care enough about your gifts to get there.

Nothing Of Substance
Happens From The Outside

"The inner struggle defines your wingspan. You just can't know that kind of flight without that kind of fight. You just can't know the glory of the other side until you've almost died."
A journal entry

~

"More than someone who has made it 'big,' we admire someone of magnitude; that individual faced her smallness and self-imposed repression, and laughed at limitation for all of us."
A journal entry

*M*aybe you wish you could shortcut the sweat, grime, and doubt, and slip through paradise's back door where the emcee hands you your check, your prize, your adoration, and your sports car, *now*. Okay, so I had a few fantasies myself. I thought it would be nice to avoid all the trouble and just fast-forward to the juicy part when I'm signing books and waving from the float in the parade.

The truth is, I used to obsess over how unfair it was that I didn't know anybody who knew anybody who could just publish me and save me the despair of agonizing over whether I would actually make it. But one day when I turned avocado green because another beginning writing buddy had "a contact" at a publishing house and I didn't, I spit into my journal and my heart responded: *"Nothing of substance happens from the outside,"* it said. "You can give someone an opportunity, a job, even a blank check, but you can't bestow a real achievement."

It took me a while to understand this real achievement thing. But here's how it goes. The hero's journey *creates* the hero. Heroes don't skip steps, bribe the bouncer, or jet off to lush destinations. That's tourism. Heroism doesn't mark a change in position—but a change in self. Real achievement occurs in our energy, in our chemistry, and in the way we hold ourselves even when no one else is looking. Of course, someone can plop us at the peak of the pinnacle, but that doesn't give us the big beaming soul and blossoming dignity to stand there. Everyone knows that a fluted bottle doesn't make a fine wine.

Over the years, I've cornered happy, fruitful entrepreneurs or artists, and begged them to share their stories, theories, fantasies, and follies. Same story every time. They didn't suck bloated cherries at cocktail parties, and guzzle and nuzzle up to "important" people in their attempt to glom on to notoriety and influence. Instead of following idols around, they followed their heart's hunches, and hung by a strand of steadfastness or, sometimes, a line of credit. And gradually, these homespun lurches and reaches grew into expertise and a succulent faith in life and self. Success followed like a lovesick school girl. These audacious startups became "important" people in their own place and time.

For example, Catelyn, now a children's therapist with a wait-ing list of clients, said she "dropped out" for five years to put a career of nursing behind her and heal her aching heart. "I encountered my own pain head-on, my judgments, terrors, and condemnations, and when I decided to surface in the world again, I was strong from the inside out," she says. Having stood up to her demons, stared into their bloodshot orange eyes and shrugged off their raspy negativity, she stole their fire for herself. Catelyn's strength can't be fabri-cated—or ignored. It glitters in her eyes and magnetizes a clientele.

"I didn't have any guarantees so I had to push myself harder," says Scott, who started his own greenhouse after leaving a job in sales. "I flew by the seat of my pants and I learned things no one could have taught me. People can give you advice, but they can't give you knowledge. You have to earn knowledge." Scott's first-hand experience adds a genuineness to his service and a sea-soned quality that customers can sense.

Eventually, I began to realize that even if a beneficent Madison Avenue editor or a fairy godmother could publish me, he or she could not make me a gifted writer. No one on Cloud Nine had anything they could hand down out of mercy, recklessness, or even pity. Sure, they might have a connection. But they couldn't engineer a self-connection, the most important ingredient of a gleaming life. They could give me a chance, but they couldn't pro-vide me with my will or my wings. No one else could possibly give me the ability to sit down in a lonely room with a mind full of self-accusation and mind the flutes and harps of my love instead. Only I could pluck those notes. Only I could open my heart and channel my love and expression into enterprise and art.

Of course, it's hard not to want to look for a way *out* of the way *through*. But this much I know: every genuine tear contains magic healing properties. We actually need some frustration, exaspera- tion, doubt, self-criticism, desire, and rage. This kind of soul-feuding hurtles us spin- ning out of our bodies so we can't ever squeeze back into our tiny, familiar selves. Our hurdles will stop us, enrage us, and engage us, until we summon a wild power from the bowels of the will we did not know we had. Then we can never again mask our magnificence, even to ourselves. Only death and birth will take us there.

> Heroism doesn't mark a change in position
> —but a change in self.

Others can hand you their power, but they can never hand you yours.

Transformation of any kind always exacts a holy tussle. The newborn butterfly struggles to open its wings so it can con- jure up the strength to fly. So, too, with artists, inventors, mystics, and entrepreneurs.

Rise. In the fight and flight of transformation, we become pure of heart, strong of gift, and furiously alive; we meet, heal, love, forgive, receive, and complete ourselves.

Showing Up Always Shines

"Any transforming achievement involves delving into the
reaches of ourselves, facing our sink holes and inconsistencies.
The demons do not belong to the project we choose or even
the stage of a particular endeavor; we bring the demons with us.
If I give up on writing, I'll face doubt elsewhere:
boredom, frustration, and my frail and fickle confidence.
My limitations will limit me until, once and for all,
I go all the way with a goal."
A journal entry

"The quality of the result itself means little compared to
the quality of our ability to produce results."
A journal entry

*I*f there's one conversation I've had with myself a hundred times, it runs as follows: "I'm afraid to sit down and write because I'm afraid of flat and limp words, crappy sentences, writing in need of an emergency room team. I hate to see my failure before me." Suddenly I want to brush again my already bald cat or catch that sale on men's socks at Target except I don't know a single bare-footed man. Evidently I want to flee. It's not exactly fun to face your own sense of powerlessness.

Here's the thing, though. Facing powerlessness gives you power. "Sit," says my inner guidance. "Showing up always shines." I pen these wonderful things in flower-covered journals. "Oh sure," I say to my heartless heart that wheedles me for faith and feats despite my opinion that I'm just reaching for carrots that dangle from the Milky Way or Pluto. But sometimes I sit down and "shine" even though I'm groaning and scraping through the motions.

Going through the motions does burn through the haze and anguish of letting myself down. William Blake once wrote, "He who desires but acts not, breeds pestilence." Motion shows me I'm capable of motion when I've already started developing some myth in my head about how I will never again move from the couch and the tabloids will snap my picture for their article "Most Futile Woman on Planet Discovered Existing on Chenille Loveseat." One humble step leads to dignity and even to hope and renewed interest. Eventually, sometimes many miles down the road, my innocence returns to me and I even remember that I *love* to write. At that moment, I just can't imagine why it takes so long for me to come back to this truth.

Only the work heals. The work will make you feel like working. I have a writer friend who periodically calls and says she's depressed. "I don't know, it's like this low self-esteem thing," says my usually obnoxiously buoyant friend. "Are you writing?" I ask, as though it's a spontaneous question that just fluttered into my mind like an oak leaf. And then she laughs. And I do, too. We don't need her to answer. Her sadness calls her to remember her joy. Otherwise she might just tell herself it's okay not to take steps toward the dream pounding on the doors of her heart like a fireman in the night.

I think life gives us those little appointment cards like dentists send out to remind us to get our teeth cleaned every six months. A neglected work inside us sends out despondent signals like the desire to wail in the middle of the day, eat too many cookies and their wrappers, or call that bewitching and baffling guy who was really no good for us and still hasn't left his wife. They are the flares our soul sends up during overcast nights lost at sea. They remind us to come home. They remind us to eat of the only food that can answer our strange and relentless hunger.

We are drowning when we are disregarding the mission within us. The longer we wait, the more we feel that unbearable weight. Yes, sometimes not working is just a call to rest and we really do need the rest. And sometimes it's a call to incubate bigger dreams or a more startling plan.

But you know what just plain old avoidance feels like. It's that yucky stuff at the pit of your stomach and rest won't make it go away and new ideas won't come within ten feet of you. It's quicksand and fast-bonding Super Glue, black ink, and nausea all rolled into one. Avoidance likes to tell you that it's saving you pain by keeping you from the one thing that will make you feel better.

Do the one thing. Face your work. Small deeds build strength. Take the tiniest step you can imagine toward your dream and you're back on track. Even five minutes can wheel destiny around. Five minutes of devotion equals five minutes of ascendance over pestilence and shame.

Do anything toward your dream and you will probably unleash the motivation to do more. The re-entry gives us intimacy with our craft. We remember its smell and its warmth. Our sense of mission gets tweaked. The juices flow. *Application leads to inspiration.* We stir the pot of soup and then the aroma tempts us and beckons us to cook.

Even failed attempts give feedback and knowledge. You either produce a

> **Only the work heals.**
> **The work will make you feel like working.**

perfect product or a perfect lesson. Or else you lie on the couch and wonder why your life feels empty and sad while, all the while, you know the truth and eating mounds of cheesecake doesn't change it. Avoidance just avoids all the freedom and fulfillment you deserve.

Give three hundred seconds to your dream. Take a tiny step with big integrity. It takes a step to break into a run. The result at hand doesn't matter. The resolve does. Show up for your love. Showing up always shines.

In The Present Moment
The Momentous Presents Itself

"At any instant the sacred might wipe you with its finger.
In any instant the bush may flare, your feet may rise,
or you may see a bunch of souls in a tree."
Annie Dillard

⌒

"The innocent come to work with loose shoulders and easy minds.
The innocent do not need today to make up for all the shame
they have about yesterday. They come without their yesterdays.
They do not use the new day to battle ghosts."
A journal entry

*S*ometimes working with our own creativity takes us down the road to enlightenment about as much as any other practice or discipline. It seems like it really is an art to do art of any kind.

Every guru or mystic I know will tell you that heaven awaits you in this present moment. I will tell you the same thing about inspiration. I don't care how long you've worked on a particular project or endeavor. Start new in this breath. Clear the fishnets in your mind that carry yesterday's catch and debris. Creativity doesn't give a fig about history.

A holy bliss-filled brush with magnitude demands that we drop our assumptions as we once again approach our computers, today's phone calls, the canvas, classroom, or boardroom. In deference to the power we approach, we shed our saga, our discouragement, our battered attitudes, and every one of our expectations with their rigorously tabulated score sheets and rap sheets. Today, right now, even with the project that has you feeling as though a fifty-pound sack of potatoes has crushed your butterfly heart, consider the possibility that *something uncanny can occur*. Do not underestimate the presence of love.

Emerson put it this way: "The power which resides in him is new in nature, and none but he knows what that is which he can do, nor does he know until he has tried." Creativity defies predictability. You never know when your heart will open and unleash a thousand rivers you didn't know you had. Let's face it. You don't know what you have. That's the fun and dumbfounding part of this journey. We don't really know the nature of our own soul-driven capabilities. We discover them just as soon as we bang into a steel wall and drop our old bag of tricks. After all, that's what those steel walls are for.

Have you ever watched a lake? You will never see the same water twice. It sits gray and still, then flares with ripples or dapples with sunlight. There are many lakes to every lake. So, too, with creative work. We never sit down to yesterday's job. Our work lives and breathes with a life of its own. Movement can transpire as suddenly as a grasshopper in a patch of petunias or a shadow across the moon. But we have to approach our undertakings with a curious mind, not that poorly ventilated "I know how this is going to be" mind. Suffocating minds only listen to their own opinions about how it's going to rain all day, and then do not step out on the front porch of real and exposed experience.

It doesn't matter what you didn't accomplish yesterday. It doesn't matter that you haven't looked at your project for over a week or a month, or that you abandoned it like a piece of fruit in the back of the refrigerator and it has now grown spores and a small apartment complex for micro-organisms.

> You never know when your heart will open and unleash a thousand rivers you didn't know you had.

It doesn't matter that you think nothing will ever change or go right again and everything you touch will turn to mold instead of gold. Just come back again. Visit the lake. The lake will give you truth.

Our creativity prevails again and again, in its own wanton way, and in its own immediate and casual time. I have come back to my writing with teeth clenched and eight-hundred-pound feet. Yet all of a sudden it's as though a lion crouches down at the computer and types in fierce and clear roars. I may have been blocked the day before or even the entire week before.

But suddenly I am thundering through the jungle with muscles, bulk, and a mane to die for. Sentences and gazelles and flocks of birds don't stand a chance before my raw strength and euphoric immortality. Meanwhile, the day before, a soft breeze could have disintegrated me.

It doesn't make ordinary sense. But something gives, loosens up, or steps forward like a beautiful woman in a silk sari who has been there all along, silent and amused. I have never yet figured out a formula, technique, incantation, or prayer to make this amazing transition happen. All I know is it can happen at any time. The solid and unforgiving can disappear in an instant and I am on a flying carpet in undiscovered territory, happily and delightfully wrong again in my assumptions. And always I am grateful I came back to my work. Because I did not come *back* at all; I came *forward.*

I invite you to step across the bright and beckoning threshold before you. Open a small window in your mind. Oh, sure, resistance will tell you nothing will ever be different; it's a granite wall with no way past and you might as well turn back and save yourself the dreadful pain of lifting a pinkie, lifting your hopes, or lifting your vibration. But resistance gets a sick kick out of convincing us to actually *choose* our own inertia and pain. And it's our job as wonder workers to know there are no such things as granite walls in this work—only lakes, only light beams, only the fluctuating patterns of an emotional kaleidoscope.

Jump into your work all over again. See what the tide has brought in. Something uncanny can occur today. Dive into the mystery, into the lake, into the fire and the living. Something original occurs every day.

Catch On Fire and the World Will Catch On to You

Chapter Eight

*H*ey, what about the commercial aspect in all this?" you may begin to wonder. Which means, of course, you assume that if you just "followed your heart" you'd sit in your room and generate fitful and irrelevant works, and nobody would ever know about you until they found your bones.

Okay, you do have to leave your room—because that gives grace some operating room.

But you don't have to "find" your way. You don't know the way. Just enter the world as one who shares what he or she has been given. Share generously and zestfully. Each encounter strengthens you, broadcasts your abilities, and feeds your heart's fire.

Feed the fire. Burn pure and bright. And the world's opportunities will draw close to your love, talent, and service like moths drawn to the light.

Just Start Dancing And
The Band Will Find You

"I don't need a paycheck to give myself permission to work
*toward **my** goals. The market pays for mastery and professionalism,*
not potential. If an editor ever asks, 'So, what have you got?'
I don't want to mumble, 'Nothing yet. I've been waiting for you.'
When that 'ship comes in,' I'll be at my dock,
Gucci bags in hand, ready to cast off."
A journal entry

"I know I've never said, 'Oh, bummer, I just had the universe flood
me with bliss, meaning, and purpose in my life, but you know
it sucks because nobody paid me for my time.'"
A journal entry

I don't know a better way to march our dreams into the world
other than to just march our dreams into the world. You could wait
for the world to invite you to the banquet and the ball. Or you could
just show up in your red dress and your headdress ready to boogie.
I think the red dress is in order. The universe has invited us all to
thrive in our lives and no one and nothing is ever holding us back.

I know so many creative soul friends who cloister their
abilities like pearls in oyster shells beneath the sea, praying, hoping, sinking, aching, and waiting, waiting, waiting. They wait for

their chance like some kind of leprechaun to appear in the tall grasses with an embossed invitation from the queen. You *are* the queen. And it's not chance that creates our chances.

You have enough opportunities to share, showcase, and refine your talents right in the here and now. Belt out your song over the baked beans at the company picnic *now*, paint postcards to your friends, practice telling your stories at the Jewish nursing home where somebody's mother sleeps in loneliness for most of the day, interview a fascinating person for your community newspaper, or design a web site for a firecracker organization you believe in. Tiny actions taken with huge-heartedness awaken fortuitous breaks and breakthroughs. Some of the richest opportunities await in the plainest of circumstances.

Fling those precious pearls like dandelion seeds to the breeze. Let life get wind of you. Sharing your gifts invigorates and promotes them. Talents intensify with use. Meanwhile, guarding your gifts keeps them in the dark where they do not grow or glow. Waiting until "the right time" usually means waiting in your sea cave until you have achieved artistic perfection in this lifetime— which you will never do. This can make it tricky to attract a clientele. Yes, there is a time to go inward. But then comes the time to no longer hide your love.

Alice, a former nurse and budding photographer, says she realized one day that *National Geographic* wasn't going to ship her off on safari until she logged some mileage on her own khakis and camera. So she assigned herself an expedition, shooting cactus flowers in the dawn of a California desert. She bought an airline ticket, a dozen rolls of film, and a journal with a sunrise on the cover. Later, she titled and matted and framed the prints as though they were destined for gallery walls. She labeled them with her biography and vision statement, and distributed them as Christmas presents to family, friends, and some acquaintances. Alice presented her art as *art* instead of as an apologetic hobby she'd stuffed in her closet and hid from the world's awaiting embrace.

Months later, an assistant to a travel magazine editor studied a photograph she liked in the bathroom of her hairdresser's house at a New Year's Eve party. Three months later, the editor of the magazine gave Alice an assignment and a reason to believe in a destiny filled with sunrises. "Did you ever observe to whom the accidents happen? Chance favors only the prepared mind," noted scientist Louis Pasteur.

Years ago, when I decided to start creativity coaching, I sweet-talked a few acquaintances, even begged and bribed some, to sit with me on my seen-better-days beige couch and let

> Fling those precious pearls like dandelion seeds to the breeze. Let life get wind of you.

me practice my seedling magic on them. I just couldn't wait to help creative people honor their inspired dreams. Yet throughout each session, *I* flourished when our work together unlocked a hidden wonder. My experimentation matured into expertise, confidence, and even more enthusiasm for the work. Later, these "clients" became walking advertisements for me that attracted *real*, non-bribed business. I started an entrepreneurial momentum by starting to give of my gifts in every moment I could.

So can you. Start somewhere, anywhere, and the dynamism of heartfelt action will take you to the next destination. Just hop on the train. Our world needs your sensibilities and original abilities, your caring hands, and customized pipeline to the infinite and sublime. There are whispers and pleas in the air calling your name. Please don't hold yourself back any longer, waiting in isolation for your invitation. The hours that you "give away" will give you back some peacock feathers in your cap, hands-on training, a spiral notebook of contacts, fire in the belly, smoke signals in the heart, and friends in the field. You just can't beat that rate of exchange.

So gorge yourself on experience. *Experience is power.* Experience is exposure. Experience leads to experience that leads to expertise and glowing auras. And, boy, when you're talking glowing auras, there's no telling what you'll attract after that.

It's easier than you think to assume your place in the world.

Opportunity always rushes to experience. And we can give ourselves experience at any moment—by giving of our gifts.

Love Is Your License
And Your Highest Credential

"Love belongs on the résumé. It is the highest credential."
A journal entry

⌒

"When a seven-year-old runs up to show you a pebble, you see a different pebble by looking at her face. An ordinary rock will mesmerize you in the presence of someone enlivened."
A journal entry

As I shuffled through the class catalog of Colorado Free University (CFU), an ad leapfrogged off the page onto the lily pad of my brain: "Adult education teachers wanted: computers, cooking, creative writing. . . ." *Creative writing.* I flushed. Who wouldn't want to teach creative writing? My heart flurried like that of a teenager on a date at the movies. "Forget it," I told myself. "That peach is out of reach." Me, without teaching experience or an education degree. Nothing to offer. Just mad desire.

A week later, I attended the free workshop CFU presented to spell out the goals and direction of the university. Midway through the evening, our host and leader paused and grinned. "Now, let's go around the room," he said, "and I'd like each of you to stand up and tell us about your proposed course and your teaching background."

I practically fell out of my metal folding chair. I had expected the kind of workshop where you could just hang back and let the big fish do the talking. Like watching a movie from the back row. Now, before long, the movie projector would blaze a spotlight on me. Ambush.

A woman in a navy suit and pumps began. Words streamed from her mouth like a parade, with phrases like floats and tambourines and trombones for credentials. A man in a tweed sports jacket followed. He could have sold us alligator-infested marshland and tinfoil townhouses for no money down, much less his simple little jazz course. And so the evening continued.

> The gleam in our eyes and the beam in our hearts mean even more than the diplomas and paperwork behind us.

One by one, every prospective teacher in the lineup flaunted course titles, concepts, file folders, organization plans, and starry qualifications. With my turn approaching, I wanted to duck into the ladies room and bury myself with paper towels or, better yet, crawl under one of the tiles. What would I say? I had no outline, no sales pitch, and no clue. I had just wanted to teach creative writing because of that coaxing ad and the frog on my brain and the candle in my heart.

Forcing myself to stand up, heart stammering, I mouthed a few sentences as striking as brown paper bags. "I think it would be fun to teach creative writing. I used to be a lawyer and I gave up my practice to write. It's great fun. Writing is fun, lots of fun." Mumble, mumble, pause, mumble. I glanced at the kind faces in the room, then slid back down and shriveled in my seat. For the rest of the evening, no matter how tightly I hugged my sweatshirt or jeans, I felt naked in my folding chair and billowing with cellulite.

How many times had I said the word "fun?" The writer—the wordsmith who wanted to teach others—couldn't express herself in words. Tears threatened not to wait until I could get home, bolt the door, smear my mascara, and gurgle in privacy. How silly of me to think I might get a job teaching creative writing just because I loved to write. That night, I stuffed the information into my knapsack and hurried home to a hot bath, trying to scrub myself clean of the ordeal.

Believe it or not, I applied anyway, proposed a course, and appeared for the routine interview. I tried to convince myself that maybe some of the other applicants had died or were so fantastic they had already found other positions—like teaching at Oxford, editing *The New York Times*, or running for president.

As we talked in her office crammed with books, papers, and an insistent printer, Ellen, the university's program coordinator, beamed at me. "I have instructions to hire you," she said. Instantly I found myself reeling with the weight of my crown and ermine cape, winner of the pageant. "At last week's workshop, every staff member unanimously agreed you should teach with us. We concurred on just three people out of fifty."

I continued to grip my chair, proof of three-dimensional reality. Why? What had the hiring committee seen? What could they have heard?

Fun. Fun. Fun. Fun.

I'm still not convinced that a troop of angels didn't visit the workshop, plucking harps behind me, putting on light shows, and promising heavenly dispensations to staff members as I rambled on. But I'm willing to believe that love advertises itself in bold and mysterious ways. Because over and over, I've seen inspiration gleam and hypnotize people into going an unexpected mile beyond ordinary procedures or prerequisites. Love outranks the rules.

Years after I began teaching at CFU, Ellen confided in me, "When I hire instructors, I don't put much weight on experience. I look for the spark in the teacher. That spark will ignite a classroom." Then and now, I am grateful for her insight. I don't think she's alone in that kind of insight either. We tend to underestimate the underground magnetic power of our love and commitment. But honest passion shines like sunlight in a room and trumpets on the subliminal airwaves: "This is the one, this is the one, this is the one who has the energy and devotion."

The gleam in our eyes and the beam in our hearts means even more than the diplomas and paperwork behind us. It's nice to have the right qualifications. But there is no higher qualification than genuine inspiration.

Trust the spark. Where you find your natural exuberance, you will find security. A sparkling heart attracts interest and opportunities and beams out messages that no résumé ever could. "This is the one, this is the one who has the energy and devotion," chants and whispers your enthusiasm.

The ordinary pales before the fire of genuine excitement. Love shines and even blinds—or maybe some darling cherubs do the hokey pokey behind you and make everything all right. Either way, your spark will blaze the way, enchant the gatekeepers, and save the day.

Never Mind Marketing: Hit The Mark

"The free mind goes directly on target as an arrow. It is not caught in the gravitational field of some other person; it has no need to deviate and manipulate someone."
Willard and Marguerite Beecher

⌒

"To believe your own thought, to believe that what is true for you in your private heart is true for all men—that is genius."
Ralph Waldo Emerson

One Thursday I lunched with Ralph, who owned an art gallery with a collection of cactus-and-coyote-painting artists. It was frequented by a clientele who always seemed to wear leather pants and at least eighteen silver bracelets. Naturally we got around to talking about the book I had been writing and writhing with earlier that morning. He listened with interest, stroking his black-and-silver beard. The lines on his forehead deepened. "Who's your publisher?" he asked.

Silence. "I thought I'd write the book first," I said. Ralph stabbed his fork into his salad. A cucumber jumped. "You can't do that," he said. More silence. I might as well have said, "I'm climbing a wooden ladder to the moon. I'm running for president on a campaign of bubble gum wrappers. I'm learning how to speak to Martians via the Internet."

"What?" he responded. "You have to sell a publisher on the idea ... get an aggressive agent ... a contract, an advance." The lecture. The litany. Leaning back in my chair, I could feel all the muscles in my body grit their tiny little muscle teeth, while I smiled my "I'm so interested" smile just the same. I hated these "right way to proceed" speeches. I already knew I was careening down a highway without headlights, a map, or a hotel reservation. But I had few reservations and no alternatives.

In the beginning of my writing days, I'd wanted to obey the "how to get published" books, write query letters and sample chapters, jump through the hoops, cross my tees, dot my i's, cross my legs, cross my heart and hope to die. But I couldn't. Words just boiled within me, not books, not chapters, not formal outlines or proposals, just inspiration soup. Intuitively, I knew that a recognizable form would emerge from the broth, but I couldn't tell what, or in which century. So I said a tentative yes to the mystery because nothing else had even come close to working for me.

And often I cringed to think of myself as a "temperamental artist," reckless, adamant, dream-headed, and out of touch. Truth is, I craved commercial recognition.

But I'd found that all my sentences had the sex appeal of cardboard when I tried to dress them for success. It seemed I had to discover my words, spill and tumble them, collect paragraphs and pages as if placing china bowls beneath a waterfall. I was a beggar to the muse's insolent grace. And this is what I learned: *If I wanted life in my work, I had to allow my work a life of its own.*

One day, an answer showed up in my journal. "Ignore the guesswork of marketing. Follow your conviction. Love sells." With both trepidation and relief, I abandoned pragmatism in favor of magnetism; I began to trust the tidal wave within me. Somehow, I began to *know* that my allegiance to my love would not fail me. The power of love would exude the radiant and rare, and compel an audience and a market share.

> If I wanted life in my work,
> I had to allow my work a life of its own.

Face it, marketing strategies depend on pleasing other people. Your calling depends on pleasing yourself. You can't listen to statistics and inspiration at the same time. You can look for a snug harbor in the opinions of other people—or you can find protection in your genius. But absolute genius requires absolute heart.

"If you follow someone else's way, you are not going to realize your potential," says the advocate of "follow your bliss," Joseph Campbell. And if you knew your potential, you would laugh at your efforts to fit into smaller molds.

No one can touch the true country and white light of inspiration for a false goal. You can't dive into the deep-down, belly place of pure creativity while peeking over your shoulder to monitor the preferences of strangers. Psychologist Alfred Adler referred to this division of psychic energy as "trying to chase two rabbits at once and catching neither." We either follow inner direction or external suggestion. Or we split our pants and our power.

Besides, those who survey "the market" consider the world that has already materialized—the known, the passing, and the passé. But the visionary and the mystic and the artist do not conform. They touch the next realm and return to inform. Creative energy whispers "edge" energy, the next collective movement and direction. For my dime, I'd follow the exciting more than the exiting.

Don't pressure yourself to target a market. Hit the mark instead. Pay homage to your own connection. Quantity flocks to quality and quality comes from purity. Purity wails. Integrity taps a nerve. Inspiration slips beneath the skin of your skin and turns disinterested strangers into warm-bodied kin.

Haven't you heard a song or read a line and immediately identified with the artist? "Oh yes, me too. I'm so glad someone else in this universe feels that way." Or haven't you thought to yourself, "This is just what I've been waiting for" when a clever product made it to the shelves?

We will pay for immaculate expression. We will honor the one who listened. We recognize and salivate before the truth. Our own lives jump out at us from the canvas; the actress cries our banished tears; the curve of a pot opens a door in our heart.

Listen to your desires and thousands will hear themselves. Express your individuality and it reverberates with universality. Your own will find you. But first you must sound the call. *You* must find you. Why guess at what other people prefer? You *know* the notes of your song. No other song will do. No other expression expresses you.

Your love will lead you to completion and transcendence. You don't need anything else after that. But tolerate the masses throwing their money at you anyway. And make sure to tease the know-it-all, right-way-to-proceed Ralphs of the world for good measure—and for me.

You Will Never Know The Way, But Go All The Way

"I never understood how moths could soar into flames. Now I do.
The calling turns irresistible. You don't care what happens.
Even the heat of fire is better than the cold and silent
death of holding yourself back."
A journal entry

⁓

"Sometimes I feel at home in the dance, and other times
I wonder whatever possessed me to crawl out on the highest limb
of this towering tree. It's like waking up from a dream. I think the
only answer is to get possessed again, and keep dancing."
A journal entry

*I*nevitably some "real world" event will challenge you, convince you that you are delusional rather than inspired, definitely dancing to a tune of your own, and alone in all the universe with no hope of success or redress. The mind can always find eight thousand reasons to turn back. And maybe you don't have one good "reason" to go forward. Then one day it just doesn't matter anymore. You give up the thought that you will take your dream into the world in ways you know. Now you are most pliable and magical. And that's a fine day. Because now you are willing to let the torrent of instinct float you *all the way.*

My day came when I wandered into Journey Books for a little Sunday afternoon diversion. Puttering through the aisles and sampling titles, I noticed a section marked Work/Purpose. The section intrigued me and also yanked an invisible chain. Just how many books existed on this subject, *my* subject? I hesitated before the shelf of probable snipers of my self-worth. Other authors' work, particularly validated work, could easily convince me I'd been chasing fairy dust, and I wouldn't have a place in the universe carved out and reserved for me after all.

And sure enough, propped up on a plastic display, sat a book I'd never seen before. New and exactly on my topic. My heart thumped as I held the glossy threat in my damp and eager hands. My eyes couldn't eat pages quick enough, savage with desire to locate at least one itsy-bitsy rotten passage, stupidly obvious point, or fatal flaw. Yet everything I skimmed increased my mounting horror; words bearing my message paraded across the pages like homecoming queens in sequin gowns waving to adoring crowds.

My heart sank like a stone in a lake. It's done. It's said. It's on the bookshelves. The author even had a Ph.D. And a foreword by a famous person, someone like the president, and about two thousand endorsements on the back cover. Who needs an unknown author to say the same thing now with maybe a faltering endorsement from her mother?

I flew out of the bookstore and into my apartment, slammed the door, and threw myself onto my bed wondering if I could fall asleep for the next few centuries and make all of life go away. But I felt this fish hook in my heart, a question mark I had to face and answer. Should I continue writing my book? *Of course I should.* Of course?

My mind scrambled for positive ways to see this situation. Okay, I don't have to assume a negative outcome: what if work/purpose was the hottest issue of the decade and the market couldn't buy enough writing on the subject? Or what if writing this book simply provided a stepping-stone to another book or career or layer of nirvana I couldn't yet imagine? And remember writing for the sweetness and healing it offered in the moment? *Yeah. Yeah. Yeah.* All true. But all so much costume jewelry from over the counter. I needed a sapphire from the quarry of my soul.

So I journaled wildly, writing big, loopy, desperate sentences. What's my choice here? Not do the only thing I want to do with my life? And if so, why? Because I saw another book on my topic and now I didn't believe that Oprah would beam me onto her show? Did outcome even matter?

It just didn't make sense to believe that everything had gone this right, only to go sideways now.

Then an even bigger question came sweeping in like the gust of wind that pushes the wildflowers in meadows to their thin green knees. *What about the outcome of giving up?* Dying inside. Denying my insides.

Then I began to write one word in my journal over and over again: Trust. Trust. Trust. Trust. And suddenly, oxygen began to return to my brain and the wildflowers sprang back up and frolicked in the sun.

I turned a corner that day. I hit what I called the "must" level. The last marble of wariness had rolled away. I had to trust. Only trust would let me move on. I felt like I was on some kind of train speeding a hundred miles an hour and I just couldn't get off now. I couldn't pull the brake cord or ask the conductor to slow down and pull over. I didn't want to stop. I didn't want to go back. This journey had already taken me through landscapes of the heart I'd never known before. My old life of black and white had swooped into prisms of color and light.

"Oh, I'll never forget this—this is so right—I'll never doubt again" I'd sworn a thousand times before, but you know how those promises go. Some "real world" challenge would arise, then I'd forget and squirm like a kid in the front row of a magic act, just waiting to catch a lapse in the mastery. But this time I dried my tears and closed my journal. I resolved to trust the magician more than the uproar. I'd seen enough rabbits and silver coins spring from thin air. I had danced on thin air myself—and on thin ice. It just didn't make sense to believe that everything had gone this right, only to go sideways now. I would write my book. I would stop second-guessing the wisdom of a wisdom that had carried me farther and broader than anything else ever had.

Several years later, I attended an evening lecture at a local university featuring the poet and diva of dignity Maya Angelou. Ms. Angelou said countless jaw-dropping things that evening. But I remember most her talking about her own decision to trust at a difficult time in her life. She said in her beautiful, booming voice, *"He would not have carried me this far to let me down now."* Her words filled crevices in my bones with honey and recognition. I didn't have those words back then or Maya Angelou's thunderous relationship to the divine. But I had looked behind me at a starstrewn path and I just had to believe that the same road up ahead would lead to gleaming outcomes as well.

Love does not call us to the dance only to deny us chances. There is consistency in this journey. As in the beginning, so shall it be in the middle and the end. Love does not tempt us to leave what we know, only to leave us without direction, resources, synergy, and flow.

Trust on and move on.

You have never known the way. You will never know the way. But *the way* knows the way. Remember, love would not have carried you this far to let you down. Love moves in mysterious ways, performs beneath a haze. But this unseen magnificent power takes us all the way. It may take us away from the way we assume. But it takes us all the way.

Don't Let Frustration Rob You Of Your Culmination

*"I can't imagine how anyone ever recovers
from giving up on themselves."*
A journal entry

⌇

*"I think that to be close to something dear and to stop,
is to stop being close to yourself."*
A journal entry

Kir and I had hiked for hours in Rocky Mountain National Park and still we saw no sign of our goal, Cub Lake. My T-shirt clung to my sweaty torso, my calves complained, and my stomach growled like an old, tired panther in the zoo. We'd hiked for miles and still had not arrived.

Every now and then, I'd see a clearing ahead and rush to it, only to see a clearing without a lake. Finally I could take no more. I leaned against a rock and said to Kir, "Let's turn back. I'm exhausted. Who knows how much farther we have to go?" He peeled a banana and handed it to me for a bite, a peace offering. "Let's go just a little farther," he said.

"You said the same thing two miles ago," I complained. Kir finished his banana and looked my trooper self in the eyes. "You can do it," he said. Then he held out the real bribe, half a Hershey bar with almonds.

I adjusted my knapsack, gobbled my prize, and walked on, staring at the ground, pine needles and wildflowers like confetti sprinkling the trail. I didn't exactly skip on. I made a point of trudging, announcing my opinion of this venture with each drag and sigh.

Suddenly, not five minutes from where we had sat, the trail revealed Cub Lake. The immense, blue jewel glittered in the sunlight with thousands of stars dancing on the surface and clumps of soft green lily pads yielding lemon-yellow flowers. Its beauty stunned me like a silent chorus of angels. I couldn't imagine any sight more beautiful, nor could I have imagined how this beauty could lift me out of my body and into the secret largeness of life. I stood in silence, bowing inside myself and rising, too. "Wow," I said finally. "I would have missed this."

I recall that incident often. A promise fulfilled waited just beyond that rock, just beyond my comfortable limits, my known world, just ahead of where I frayed at my edges and almost threw in both the towel and the silver towel rack.

The realization of our dearest aspirations will frustrate and surprise us like this, too. Sometimes we're so close, maybe even just a step away, but we think we should turn back because we're so tired of turning within to tap our waning reserves. Many times writing this book, I wanted to throw down my purple pen and put up a sad white flag instead. But Cub Lake came to mind, blue and brilliant, hidden and available, and carrying the echo of my own words, "Wow, I would have missed this."

I don't have a Hershey bar with almonds to offer you, but I do have a few final words. Keep going into the unknowing. Yes, each moment takes you farther away from predictability, but draws you closer to your sacred abilities. Each step equals a commitment to believe in your soul's holy quest for recognition and expression, more than to believe in failure of any kind. That is the choice. That is always the choice.

This is your solo flight. It can hurt too much to land at your own hand too soon. Let's go just a little farther.

Around that next corner, it all awaits you.

We only know peace of mind by stepping forward. Otherwise, we are fleeing toward regret.

The moment we stop believing, we burst our own balloon, give up a minute too soon, and don't allow the confluence of destiny and genius enough creative elbowroom. Please don't let frustration rob you of your culmination.

> Yes, each moment takes you farther away from predictability, but draws you closer to your sacred abilities.

Our lives deserve work that feels like grace. Our callings deserve every bead of sweat and every tentative step. Come on, dearest. You can do this. *You must do this.*

You don't want to miss this life.

Let's go just a little farther.

An Epilogue
and a Vision

A Shout Of Victory And A Sigh Of Gratitude

Late Fragment

And did you get what
you wanted from this life, even so?
I did.
And what did you want?
To call myself beloved, to feel myself
beloved on the earth.
Raymond Carver

I know if I were reading this book, I'd probably flip to this last page first. I'd want to know whether or not the author made it, became rich and famous and good friends with Cher or Oprah. I am still working on the Oprah part, okay, every part. But meanwhile, I have "arrived" in ways I did not even think to dream.

There have been many hoorah moments for me along this path that felt like destinations unto themselves. I remember the first acceptance letter and check for a piece of writing I sold. That day I screamed so loudly in my backyard that a friend thought I had totaled the car. I howled to the skies because everyone who had ever told me how hard it was to get published was wrong in that moment and wrong for all time. I made twenty-five dollars and you couldn't have given me a pile of rubies that meant more.

I also think back to the day I moved to the mountains to begin to complete this book. I wrote at a picnic bench in a spiral five-theme notebook gazing at quiet pasque flowers and noisy blue jays, serious about my deliciousness for the first time in my whole life. I couldn't believe I'd found a way to live in my own paradise and strum the chords of a symphony for one.

Then much later, there was the time a senior partner from my old law firm read an article about my "courageous career path" in a regional law journal. The article celebrated my successful seminars and my coaching and consulting with other courageous professionals. This partner whom I had once feared and revered called to congratulate me and invite me out to a little chum-fest lunch. I enjoyed the acknowledgment, but I savored even more the fact that his blessing didn't mean as much as my own.

And then, too, there was the time I spontaneously read a chapter of this book out loud at a retreat and felt the room grow quiet and full at the same time. I sensed awe in the room and applause in the silence. Everything in me shivered with completion and blatant recognition.

And, of course, the first radio talk show featuring me as some kind of expert. And buying my first sweet house, with its wood stove and exposed brick, with money I'd made doing the work I love, and so many more moments.

And while these mean the world to me, there's something underneath them all, some secret song that crests in a greater chorus still. This triumph is not one I expected or even aimed for. You could say it is the feeling of *healing*, coming home to myself after a long and bitter separation, and finding a table set with linens, candlelight, and lilacs just for me. This heart's homecoming means more to me than any publicity, paycheck, or praise. And I'm sure now that's what this whole odyssey has been about.

> **You could say it is the feeling of *healing*, coming home to myself after a long and bitter separation, and finding a table set with linens, candlelight, and lilacs just for me.**

In many paths of wisdom, there is the motif of being tricked into our destinies. I think our hearts' callings do that. We want to find a way to paint our paintings or heal the strife of others. And to do this shining work, we must leave everything we know and learn to trust in and live by grace. And somewhere down the road, living in grace becomes even more important than the original goal itself. Or maybe our real goals become more obvious.

I set out to be a writer and a workshop leader. And I craved recognition and remuneration. Well, I've landed my hand in that cookie jar. But what I didn't bargain for was the blazing hoops of personal healing I had to jump through to keep my faith alive, a faith I didn't even know I possessed. And it is these experiences of finding, befriending, and trusting myself that have become more precious to me than any particular writing or lecturing I do.

Don't get me wrong. I'm proud of what I've done. But I'm even more enthralled by who I've become.

I've become someone who trusts that, though I feel as fragile as a flaming leaf in autumn, I house the capacity of a tidal wave, a meteor shower, a white tornado of inspiration. I've become someone who believes that every human being has a tornado just beneath the skin and that we are meant to live our dreams so that we can discover that natural force within us that blows constriction away. We are meant to walk in bigger worlds. We are meant to express our love and our gifts so that we become even fuller with love and capacity.

You could say that, as artists and creative entrepreneurs, we become unwitting mystics. Through the process of creating, we personally experience the vastness, the power, the tenderness, and the vitality of an inviolable presence we did not know before, or at least not on a first-name basis. At last, we find a silver cord to a golden force that will never abandon us or deny us any good we need. We glimpse the wondrous territory of inner wholeness and the overflowing well of our own creative selves. Personally, I think that discovery is worth the whole dumbfounding journey and a Harvard law degree to boot. But you couldn't have told me that in the beginning. And I probably couldn't have told you that either.

And, yes, we'll make money. And, yes, the world will applaud. But this time there won't be emptiness when we curl up in bed at night or wake at dawn or walk the dog around the lake. Creativity comes from fullness. We are full on this path and we are free.

And we are more magical than we know. Each precious one of us has access to magnitude, a lyrical destiny, a path of epiphanies, cause for gratitude.

So, dearest, you can rest. You can trust. You can hum.

You can "lose control" and gain a life of freedom and of footing beyond compare. You can breathe and you can prance.

You can dance. You can dance. You can dance.

An Invitation To The Dance

"It is the art of mankind to polish the world, and everyone who works is scrubbing some part."
Henry David Thoreau

~

"If you do not listen to your own original ideas, if you do not listen to your own being, you will have betrayed yourself. Also, you will have betrayed our community in failing to make your contribution to the whole."
Rollo May

I invite you to this dance. We live in times that cry out for love and radical resourcefulness. We live in times that beg for new voices of bold grace. Safe choices have led us into unsafe times. An increase in diseases of exhaustion and toxicity. Pollution. Crime. And gutted spirits. We believed we needed "good" jobs. But those "good" jobs did not lead us to the goodness we desired.

It's obvious, now, that work needs to support not just our material lifestyles, but our true lives—and life, itself. We need artists, *artists in every profession*, who can lead the world love-first into the healing realms of devotion expressed.

Take up *your* love, your desire to express world beauty or bone wisdom, to cherish potential, or to devise and promote that preferable way. A universal intelligence has gifted you with a whispering wish, not to question, mock, or dilute, but to give your life to—and be given life in return.

Trust these meek and gargantuan ideas. Tend even the preposterous seed. The idea begs you. I beg you.

You do not know where love will lead.

You do not know where love will lead.

You do not know where love will lead.

Throughout the world's history, it has taken *desire*, not safe, predictable, acceptable, and impenetrable thinking, to spark cures, breakthroughs, shifts in consciousness, revolutions, and renaissances. Discoveries dawned on the minds of the ardent and engaged, the jubilant and enraged, not merely the employed. The worship of convention has never yet led to astonishment and a joyous leap in human potential. Only enthusiasm plants wild gardens in the mind and harvests inspired fruits and flowers. Only enthusiasm, born of light, conceives of brighter worlds to walk in.

What if we all followed our natural desire to share our love and creativity? Can you imagine the loving and the gifted teaching, writing, singing, selling groceries and carburetors, and leading nations and scientific and economic explorations? Can you imagine impassioned, grateful souls at corporate headquarters, in the courtroom and the newsroom, in the wheat field and the bean field, even in the operating room? If we each stood in our right places with invincible hearts and visionary minds, would we not stand in a different world? *Of course we would.* And our feet wouldn't even touch the ground.

We live in a world of infinite possibility waiting to unfold. We all have so much to give, so much secret richness encoded in the passion of our dreams. Love transforms us into healers and leaders, lights and fountains, and movers of mountains. When each of us pours our life-energy into the art, service, or industry that enlarges our existence, we will, at last, avail ourselves of the most untapped and unsung resource on the planet: *creative inspiration.*

Only enthusiasm plants wild gardens in the mind and harvests inspired fruits and flowers.

Choose to use your gifts and live the adventure of this lifetime. Step into the larger scheme of following your dream. Let's deluge the world with the ultimate dancers, people who feed their souls with work and feed their work with soul.

Soul will see us through.

Let Us Dance!

*E*very creative contribution makes its way into the world through the love of unseen hands. Thank you for being those hands. Thank you. Thank you. Thank you.

You may propel the spirit of this work forward by simply carrying a spark in your heart. You may carry it forward by reading a passage to a co-worker. You may carry it forward by spontaneously buying this book for a friend or for an army of friends. You probably know a creative soul in transition or one who *should be* in transition.

Do not underestimate the possibilities you open for others by sharing your own enthusiasm.

Here are some more powerful ways to invite creativity into our world:

1. Above all else do your dream.

2. Visit our website at **www.AwakeningArtistry.com** and continue the journey with more insight and inspiration, a schedule of talks, workshops, and retreats, information on private coaching, and other ways to stay committed to your journey; connect with visionary entrepreneurs, artists and artisans, pioneers and pilgrims, and all who endeavor to work with passion.

3. Invite me to speak at your wing of the White House, convention, conference, writers' group, or backyard barbecue.

4. Discover the magic of starting a *This Time I Dance!* group. I urge you to create support for living your dreams. You can even do this with just one friend or email buddy. Where two or more are gathered, grace rushes in with twinkling eyes. Your dream deserves a stimulating network of people who each bring different gifts, experience, and resources to the table. Visit our website for some great guidelines, discussion topics, and assignments you can use in your group. You can also list your support group with us and find out about other existing groups.

5. Please write with your feedback. I'd love to hear from you. Silence makes me nervous.

6. Do you have an idea of how to let people know about this book and related seminars, workshops, and retreats? I look forward to creative collaborations. I know you have magical spices to add to the stew.

7. Become part of our "dream team" and awaken the world to another way of working and living. We'd be happy to share our suggestions for sharing this message in your community.

8. **Stay tuned. Our dance has just begun.**

To contact **Tama J. Kieves** or to find out more about the work of **Awakening Artistry,** please contact us at:

Awakening Artistry

P.O. Box 9040, Denver, CO 80209–9040
(303) 715-0939
www.AwakeningArtistry.com

How to Create a *This Time I Dance!* Group

A group can be a commitment to a friend or an email buddy. Or it can be a blessed gaggle of like minds. There is so much power in community, shared commitments, and intentions. A *This Time I Dance!* group works for those who want to discover their passion or create the work they love. It's also a great forum for those who are already doing the work they love or expressing their creativity but want to realize a new level of passion and success. You can find the guidelines on our website, but I wanted to give you a taste of what you might focus on in a group.

SAMPLE QUESTIONS, THEMES, AND ASSIGNMENTS FOR DISCUSSION:

Chapter 1: Can love unlock extraordinary powers in us? Do you believe that it's "more practical to be magical"?

> *"We can deny our hearts or we can deny our limits."*
> *"The restrained self will always see a restraining world."*
> *"Something in us longs for the impossible because we know it's possible."*

ASSIGNMENT: Write about times in your life when you followed your love, tapped the power of your inspiration, or just felt magical.

Chapter 2: Whose values am I living? Reevaluating my life, what is my definition of success?

> *"Criticism only strikes a fire when we provide the wood."*
> *"It doesn't matter what we can buy. It matters what we buy inside."*
> *"Count on support you can't account for."*

ASSIGNMENT: Write a new definition of success for yourself. Write about what means more to you than making money or getting other people's approval.

For more questions, themes, and assignments and for further information on starting a group or existing groups, visit our website at www.AwakeningArtistry.com

Credits

With Thanks

I will never be able to thank all the people who have inspired me along the way or kept me reaching inside for my own artistry and bravery. But here I go:

I thank all creative people everywhere who have gone before me and beside me and made this walk on the high beam possible. In particular I thank all my "students" who have, of course, been my beloved friends and teachers, especially my Friday family of writers. I thank Wang Chung for all the love and comfort while writing and editing; there is no love like cat love. I thank "Wesley Craig" for a magical dance in this lifetime. I thank Donna Watson for crossing out metaphors on my manuscript and loneliness on the path. I thank Colleen Smith for joining with me in the syndrome of "women-who-can't-finish-their-books" and for teaching me how to call myself "honey." I thank Paul Kuhn for believing me when I said, "I am an organization wanting to happen" and for helping to make it happen, make it happen, make it happen. I thank all the unseen hands that have pushed me over this cliff and held me at the same time. And I thank everyone for the deep-seated generosity and spirit they hold. Amen.

About the Author

Tama J. Kieves grew up in Brooklyn, New York, and graduated from Brooklyn College *summa cum laude* as an English major. She went on to graduate from Harvard Law School *cum laude* and joined one of Denver's largest corporate law firms. There she practiced in the litigation department and earned a place on the partnership track. One summer as she sat on a California beach, eating a cinnamon-raisin bagel and watching silver waves crash, she realized that the "official track of success" would not provide her with the riches of her own true path. She left the legal practice to write and to embolden others to live and breathe their most meaningful self-expression.

Today, Kieves writes and devotes her dynamic energy to private coaching and presenting workshops and retreats nationally. Her events brim with "real world" examples, intimate attention, sharp humor, and lasting transformations. A member of the National Speakers Association, she has taught in large corporations, New Age conferences, and most everything in between. Her unique work has been spotlighted in publications and on television and radio talk shows. She is also a national presenter for A Course in Miracles,® an international program dedicated to living in love instead of fear.

Kieves now lives under the big blue skies of Denver.